SOUTH AFRICAN

GOLF COURSES

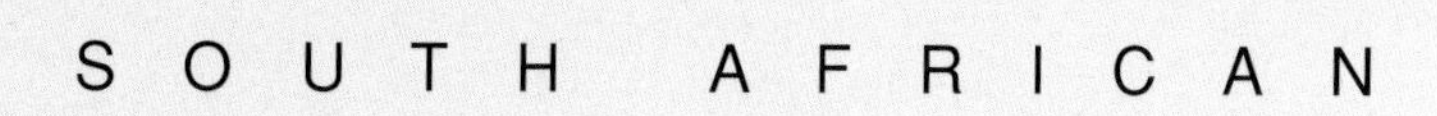

SOUTH AFRICAN

GOLF COURSES

A Portrait of the Best

STUART McLEAN

To Adrian Frederick,
who shared with me the dream of this book.

Struik Publishers
(a member of The Struik Group (Pty) Ltd)
Cornelis Struik House
80 McKenzie Street
Cape Town 8001

Reg. No.: 63/00203/07

First published 1993

Edited by Nicola Marshall
Design and DTP make-up by Kevin Shenton
Research by Hilda Hermann
Golf course illustrations by Dave Snook
Map (page 6) by Janine Blaauw

Reproduction by Unifoto (Pty) Ltd, Cape Town
Printing and binding by Leefung-Asco Printers Ltd, Hong Kong

Photography: **Herman Potgieter**: cover.
Mark van Aardt: Fish River Sun Country Club, East London Golf Club, Fancourt Country Club, George Golf Club, Humewood Golf Club, Milnerton Golf Club, Mowbray Golf Club, Royal Cape Golf Club.
Richard Wege: Durban Country Club, Maritzburg Country Club, Mount Edgecombe Country Club, Royal Durban Golf Club, Selborne Country Club, Wild Coast Sun Country Club.
Emil Wessels: Gary Player Country Club, Glendower Golf Club, Goldfields West Golf Club, Hans Merensky Golf Club, Houghton Golf Club, Maccauvlei Golf Club, Roodepoort Country Club, Royal Johannesburg Golf Club, The Wanderers Golf Club, Oppenheimer Park Golf Club, Sishen Golf Club.

ISBN 1 86825 338 4

HALF-TITLE PAGE: *The Wanderers Golf Club, Johannesburg: the 9th green with the clubhouse in the background.*
TITLE PAGE: *Fancourt Country Club, George: the par-three 6th hole.*
RIGHT: *Wild Coast Sun Country Club, Transkei: the 16th fairway and green.*

CONTENTS

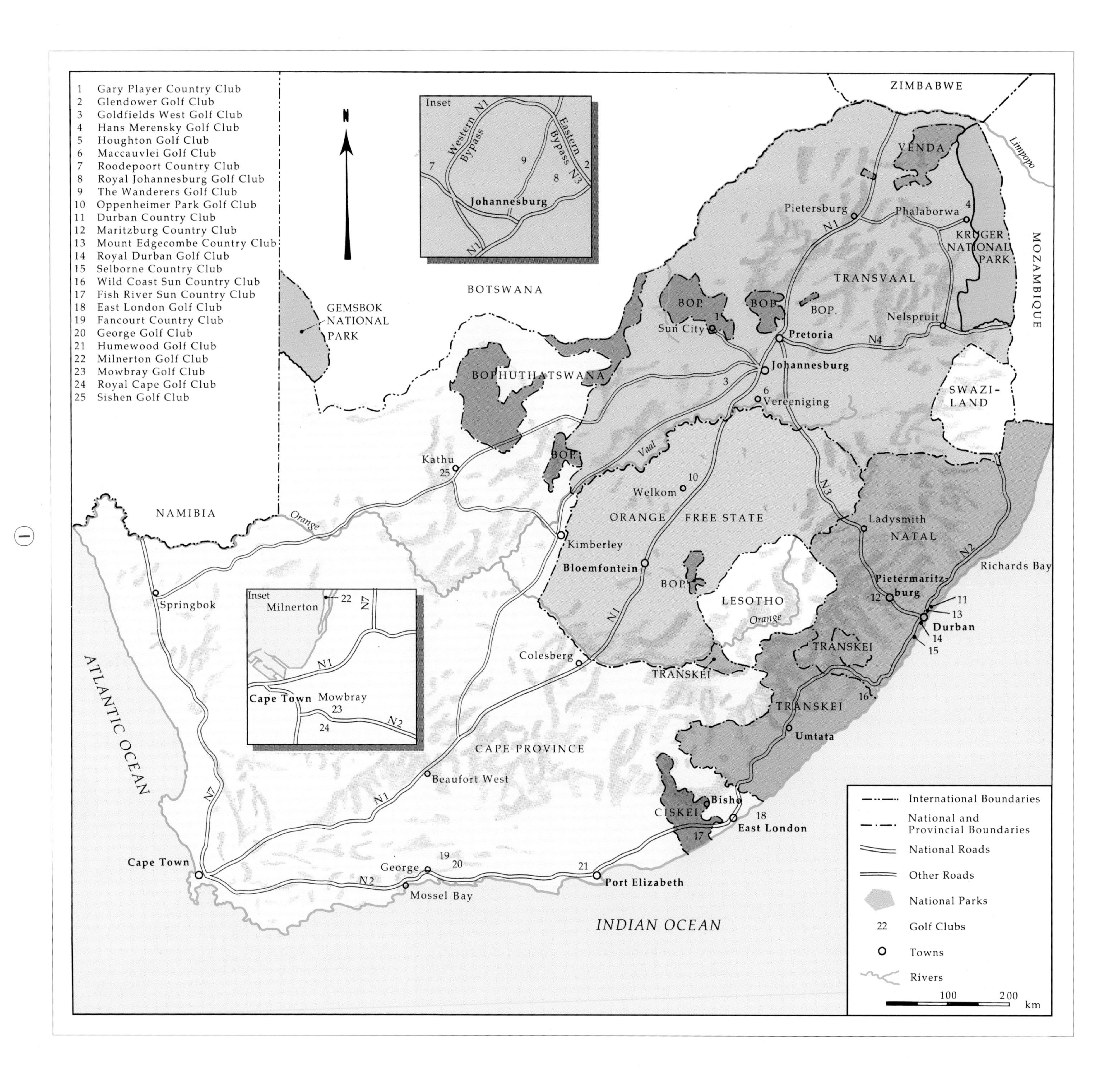
1 Gary Player Country Club
2 Glendower Golf Club
3 Goldfields West Golf Club
4 Hans Merensky Golf Club
5 Houghton Golf Club
6 Maccauvlei Golf Club
7 Roodepoort Country Club
8 Royal Johannesburg Golf Club
9 The Wanderers Golf Club
10 Oppenheimer Park Golf Club
11 Durban Country Club
12 Maritzburg Country Club
13 Mount Edgecombe Country Club
14 Royal Durban Golf Club
15 Selborne Country Club
16 Wild Coast Sun Country Club
17 Fish River Sun Country Club
18 East London Golf Club
19 Fancourt Country Club
20 George Golf Club
21 Humewood Golf Club
22 Milnerton Golf Club
23 Mowbray Golf Club
24 Royal Cape Golf Club
25 Sishen Golf Club
N
Inset
Western N1 Bypass
Eastern Bypass N3
Johannesburg
N1
ZIMBABWE
VENDA
Limpopo
Pietersburg
Phalaborwa
KRUGER NATIONAL PARK
MOZAMBIQUE
TRANSVAAL
BOTSWANA
GEMSBOK NATIONAL PARK
BOP.
Sun City
Pretoria
Nelspruit
N4
Johannesburg
BOPHUTHATSWANA
Vereeniging
SWAZI-LAND
Vaal
Kathu
Welkom
NAMIBIA
Orange
ORANGE FREE STATE
N3
Ladysmith
NATAL
N2
Kimberley
Bloemfontein
Richards Bay
Pietermaritz-burg
Springbok
Inset
Milnerton
N7
N1
Cape Town
Mowbray
N2
LESOTHO
Orange
Durban
ATLANTIC OCEAN
Colesberg
TRANSKEI
CAPE PROVINCE
Umtata
Beaufort West
CISKEI
Bisho
East London
Cape Town
George
Mossel Bay
Port Elizabeth
INDIAN OCEAN
International Boundaries
National and Provincial Boundaries
National Roads
Other Roads
National Parks
Golf Clubs
Towns
Rivers
100
200
km

INTRODUCTION

South Africa is a golfing utopia which is as yet largely undiscovered by the rest of the world. Not only do the courses compare with the finest in the world, being superb layouts in magnificent condition and built in areas of great beauty, but nearly all of them welcome visitors, they are generally uncrowded, and they promote walking rather than driving a cart. The South African climate also makes golf a year-round attraction.

Hundreds of courses stretch from the famous Cape Peninsula, where golf can be played in close proximity to the sea and Table Mountain, to the Transvaal highveld, where the dry climate was seemingly created for pleasurable golfing.

The last two decades have seen a great improvement in the conditioning of courses throughout the country. Many of them, particularly in the Transvaal, now have bent-grass greens and modern water reticulation systems, while design work has progressed in keeping with modern trends. Clubs are constantly upgrading their courses and facilities in order to present themselves as attractively as possible to a growing golfing population.

This book presents, in no order of preference, a personal selection of the 25 best courses in the country, and there are probably another 25 almost as good which unfortunately could not be included. The more famous courses are naturally featured, but selecting the rest was problematic as inevitably it is difficult to decide exactly what makes one course better than another, particularly when so many of the courses deserve recognition. New courses are also being built at an increasingly rapid pace, all of them competing for a place among the top layouts in South Africa.

Golf has been a popular game in South Africa for more than a century, the first club having been founded in the Cape in 1885, and there is a thriving professional circuit. The South African Professional Golfers' Association has held tournaments on their various tours at virtually all of the courses featured in this book.

The 25 courses featured are spread throughout the country, from the big cities of Johannesburg, Cape Town and Durban, to distant country areas such as Phalaborwa in the north-eastern Transvaal and Kathu in the semi-desert of the northern Cape. They are a mix of old and new courses; 15 were built before the Second World War, while seven have been constructed within the last 20 years.

Rating courses around the world has become a popular pastime, and some publications have it down to a fine art. The general criteria used for judging involve not only the aesthetic appeal of the course, the memorability of the holes and the satisfaction they give the golfer walking the course. A good course also has to be challenging, testing a player's all-round skills with every club in the bag. It should demand both power and finesse, and fairly reward a well-played shot.

The history of the club plays an inevitable role in rating a course. Clubs which have hosted championships have been favoured here; after all, they would not have been chosen as championship venues had they not been exacting courses.

Ten of the courses featured – Royal Johannesburg, Houghton, Glendower and Maccauvlei in the Transvaal, Royal Durban and Durban Country Club in Natal, and Humewood, Mowbray, Royal Cape and East London in the Cape Province – have staged the South African Open, the country's premier golfing event. The three Royal clubs and East London Golf Club are among the oldest in the country, all having celebrated their centenaries.

Another aspect to be strongly considered is the design of the layout: the way the holes have been routed, their variety and the utilization of the land.

Gary Player is the best known golfer South Africa has ever produced, and today he is also one of the world's foremost golf course architects. In recent years he has built new courses on a regular basis in South Africa, with the help of designer Phil Jacobs. These courses have introduced modern course design to the country, and all are of championship class. Some of them are featured in this book, while others will take their place among the best courses in the country with time.

Player's first course in South Africa was the Gary Player Country Club at Sun City, and since 1982 this has been the venue for the Million Dollar Challenge, an invitation tournament which has attracted all the great names in international golf.

Many of South Africa's more prominent older courses bear the design signature of the late Robert Grimsdell, a celebrated architect whose name is associated with several of the courses in this book. South Africa was fortunate to have a man such as Grimsdell at a time when golf was developing in the country. He was a club professional for many years and was also an excellent golfer, having been runner-up in the Opens of 1931 and 1932.

He worked solely in South Africa and Zimbabwe (then Rhodesia), and for five decades, from the 1930s to the 1970s, he designed new golf courses and updated and improved old courses. His masterpiece is Royal Johannesburg's East Course, which he designed and built during the 1930s.

Grimsdell was a close friend of Charles Hugh Alison of the British golf course architectural firm, Colt and Alison. They both settled in South Africa in the 1920s. Alison created the superb Glendower layout in Johannesburg, which is ranked among the top five courses in the country at present. He was also commissioned to make alterations at Mowbray and Royal Johannesburg golf clubs.

Other leading overseas architects who had an influence on South African courses were Colonel S.V. Hotchkin, who designed the impressive Humewood links on the eastern Cape coast, and Robert Trent Jones Junior, who created the spectacular Wild Coast Sun Country Club course.

This book pays tribute not only to the country's best golf courses, but also to the clubs which perpetuate the tradition of golf in South Africa, and to the designers whose visions resulted in the creation of these magnificent courses.

GARY PLAYER COUNTRY CLUB

Designed by Gary Player and Ron Kirby

Sun City has been influential in bringing big-time tournament golf to southern Africa with the Million Dollar Challenge. Virtually all of the greatest international players of the 1980s and '90s have competed in this invitation event which has become one of South Africa's most eminent sporting occasions. They soon found out, however, that the Gary Player Country Club course is one of the most exacting courses in the world.

Player set out from the start to design a truly great championship layout and this course, measuring 6 947 metres off the back tees, ranks as one of his best creations. For anyone who has played it, it is an unforgettable 18 holes of golf. On its completion in 1979, Player successfully demonstrated how the course could be played by winning the first tournament to be held there, the inaugural Sun City Classic, with a ten-under-par score of 278.

Situated in a hollow in the Pilanesberg mountains, the layout undulates severely. The highest point on the course is the 14th tee, which is the position furthest away from the Sun City hotel complex, providing a magnificent view across the valley encompassing all 18 holes.

The course is intimidating, but different sets of tees make it accessible to the club golfer. Stretched to its limit, however, it can only really be played

The immense bunker guarding the 14th green lies in wait for any shot that is played short.

competitively by professionals and top amateurs. Apart from the sheer length of the holes, Player designed sloping, cloverleaf-shaped greens which demand that the top players hit exact iron shots to a myriad tricky pin positions.

When built, the course presented a completely new experience for South African golfers used to conventional designs – Player having successfully introduced the American influence in golf course architecture to this country. The lure of the greatest first prize in golf attracted a host of famous golfers to Sun City and put Sol Kerzner's resort on the world map.

Distinguished major championship winners, including Johnny Miller, Raymond Floyd, Severiano Ballesteros, Bernhard Langer and Ian Woosnam, have their names inscribed on the Million Dollar Challenge trophy, while others like Nick Faldo, Greg Norman, Jack Nicklaus, Lee Trevino and Sandy Lyle have tried and failed.

The very first Challenge, played from 31 December 1981 to 3 January 1982, featured just five players and produced a stupendously exciting finish which guaranteed the future success of the tournament. Competing for the first prize of $500 000, former US and British Open champion Johnny Miller, and rising Spanish star Severiano Ballesteros, battled for nine agonizing,

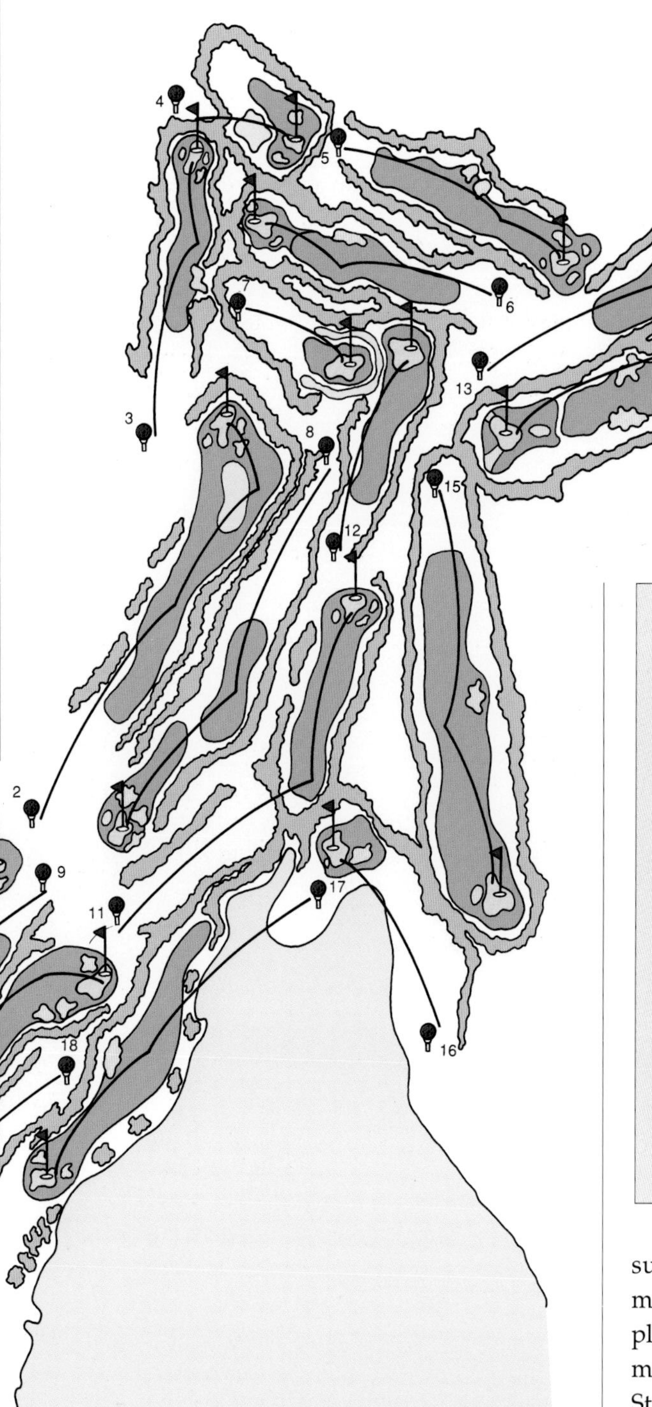

GARY PLAYER COUNTRY CLUB

HOLES 18
DISTANCE 6 947 metres
PAR 72
RATING 76

HOLE	METRES	PAR	HOLE	METRES	PAR
1	403	4	10	518	5
2	503	5	11	419	4
3	395	4	12	207	3
4	204	3	13	395	4
5	400	4	14	550	5
6	363	4	15	417	4
7	206	3	16	195	3
8	431	4	17	374	4
9	545	9	18	422	4
OUT	**3 450**	**36**	**IN**	**3 497**	**36**

sudden-death play-off holes before Ballesteros missed a short putt. In December 1982, another play-off took place with US PGA champion Raymond Floyd beating US Masters champion Craig Stadler after four sudden-death holes. The size of the field had been increased to 10 – the most it has ever been.

With tournament purses escalating around the world during the 1980s, the first prize was increased to $1-million in 1987 and competed for on a winner-takes-all basis. The first prize has

The 9th hole with its island green is a favourite with spectators during the Million Dollar Challenge.

MILLION DOLLAR CHALLENGE WINNERS

1981-2	Johnny Miller (277)*
1982	Raymond Floyd (280)**
1983	Severiano Ballesteros (274)
1984	Severiano Ballesteros (279)
1985	Bernhard Langer (278)
1986	Mark McNulty (282)
1987	Ian Woosnam (274)
1988	Fulton Allem (278)
1989	David Frost (276)
1990	David Frost (284)
1991	Bernhard Langer (272)
1992	David Frost (276)

* Won play-off against Severiano Ballesteros
** Won play-off against Craig Stadler

remained at $1-million, although since 1988 there has also been substantial prize money for the other places. The excitement of the Million Dollar Challenge for spectators is the way in which the professionals conquer – or at times stumble over – some exceptionally difficult holes.

There are three particularly tough par-fours, the 8th, 11th and 18th holes, which usually determine the outcome of the tournament. Anyone playing these holes level par or better over the four days can be considered a great shotmaker.

The 8th hole, measuring 431 metres from the championship tee, has wrecked the hopes of many competitors. The tee shot has to reach a narrow section of fairway lying in a low depression with bush on both sides, and it must finish short of a stream. The hole then slopes upwards to a green which has been cleverly concealed among bunkers. Not only is the green difficult to reach with a second shot, it has separate tiers and corners which accentuate the importance of accuracy.

The 419-metre 11th hole is a sharp dogleg-left, with a ravine which has to be carried by the tee shot. A bold drive cutting the corner of the dogleg will be rewarded with a shorter second shot to the green, but it is a dangerous line to take.

The 18th hole, at 422 metres, is a superb finishing hole – another dogleg-left with an exacting second shot that must carry a large dam. While the water may not instil as much fear in the top players as it does in other golfers, it is not the only problem to be faced. When the pin is placed at the top right-hand corner of the green, as it usually is on the final day of the Million Dollar Challenge, it takes a long second shot to carry the bunkers, which are strategically placed in a grassy mound positioned to the right of the green.

David Frost birdied the 18th hole to win the Million Dollar Challenge in 1990 by one shot from the Spaniard José-Maria Olazábal, after both had struck magnificent middle-iron second shots close to this awkward pin position.

The favourite hole for the gallery at Sun City during the Million Dollar Challenge is the par-five 9th. They gather around its large island green waiting to see who will dare to try and reach it in two shots. In every round there is sure to be drama. In 1987, Fulton Allem carded nine at this hole while leading the Challenge in the third round and immediately ceased to be a contender.

Two of the remaining par-five holes also include a number of special features. The 503-metre 2nd hole has a fairway which slopes towards a dam, while the narrow 14th green is guarded by an immense bunker ready to catch any shot which is played short of the green. Clumps of love grass within the bunker create additional hazards.

OPPOSITE: *Carved out of rugged bush, with its cloverleaf-shaped greens, tricky bunkers and water hazards, the 204-metre par-three 4th hole is typical of this exacting course.*

An aerial view of the par-three 16th hole, with the 11th fairway in the background.

No hole at Sun City can be described as easy. Even the shortest par-four off the back tees, the 363-metre 6th, has a green which is tucked away in a tiny clearing of bush. The 3rd hole is particularly attractive with its roller coaster fairway which ascends to the green.

Each of the par-three holes is characterized by steeply contoured greens but the degree of difficulty of these short holes depends on which tee is used. The picturesque 4th may be played with a short-iron from the front tee or a long-iron from the back. However, a dam lies in wait for any shot which falls short.

The par-three 16th hole is built on a corner of the main Sun City dam, although the water does not come into play. The par-four 17th hole runs alongside this dam, and is reasonably short at 374 metres. The fairway has been moulded in such a way that there is only a narrow gap between the water and a large fairway bunker for anyone attempting to take the tiger line. The small green on the 17th hole can offer some intriguing pin placements. Ian Woosnam holed his second shot with a seven-iron at this hole in the final round to win the Million Dollar Challenge in 1987.

Gary Player has recently completed the construction of a second course at Sun City, the Lost City course, which is considered to be equally as magnificent as the first. This course opened in early 1993, and the two courses together make the Sun City complex one of the finest golfing playgrounds in southern Africa.

OPPOSITE: *The narrow 17th fairway runs alongside a dam to the green, which requires an accurate approach shot.*

GLENDOWER GOLF CLUB

Designed by Charles Hugh Alison

Glendower is one of the older Johannesburg golf courses which have increased in stature in recent years. This popular golf course is situated across the N3 motorway heading east from Royal Johannesburg and Huddle Park.

Improvements to lengthen and toughen the holes, as well as the introduction of additional water hazards, have turned what was always a good course into one of the most challenging championship layouts in the country.

Although the club has hosted many professional tournaments over the years, it was only considered worthy of its first South African Open in 1989. The Open had religiously been shared between Royal Johannesburg Golf Club and Houghton Golf Club on the 14 previous occasions it had been played in Johannesburg, from the time of the Second World War onwards. The South African Golf Union took the Amateur championship to Glendower in 1987 to celebrate the club's 50th anniversary and were encouraged by what they saw. The layout was strengthened further for the 1989 Open, and the professionals were most impressed with the course they encountered. The SAGU reversed the nines for the Open to suit television coverage, but whichever way the course is played it is a severe test of ability. Only 11 players broke the par of 288 for the four rounds during the 1989 Open at Glendower.

The club spent a considerable amount of money after the Open reshaping the greens and planting

The par-three 3rd hole runs along the side of one of Glendower's dams.

GLENDOWER GOLF CLUB

HOLES 18
DISTANCE 6 317 metres
PAR 72
RATING 73

HOLE	METRES	PAR	HOLE	METRES	PAR
1	392	4	10	409	4
2	488	5	11	351	4
3	158	3	12	342	4
4	410	4	13	474	5
5	364	4	14	146	3
6	161	3	15	471	5
7	399	4	16	375	4
8	471	5	17	195	3
9	328	4	18	383	4
OUT	**3 171**	**36**	**IN**	**3 146**	**36**

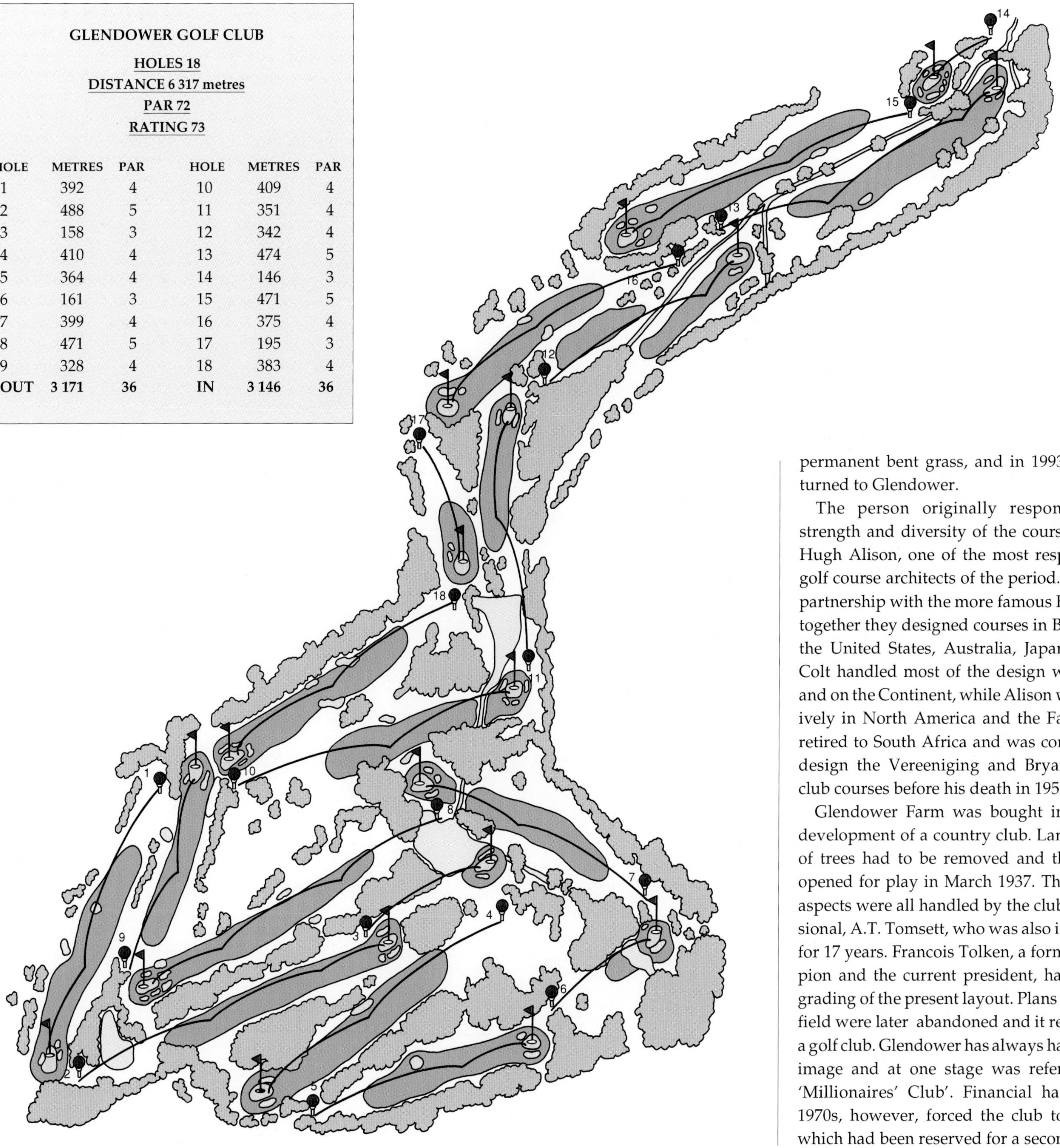

permanent bent grass, and in 1993 the Open returned to Glendower.

The person originally responsible for the strength and diversity of the course was Charles Hugh Alison, one of the most respected English golf course architects of the period. He worked in partnership with the more famous Harry Colt and together they designed courses in Britain, Ireland, the United States, Australia, Japan and Europe. Colt handled most of the design work in Britain and on the Continent, while Alison worked extensively in North America and the Far East. Alison retired to South Africa and was commissioned to design the Vereeniging and Bryanston country club courses before his death in 1952.

Glendower Farm was bought in 1935 for the development of a country club. Large plantations of trees had to be removed and the course was opened for play in March 1937. The construction aspects were all handled by the club's first professional, A.T. Tomsett, who was also its greenkeeper for 17 years. Francois Tolken, a former club champion and the current president, handled the upgrading of the present layout. Plans to build a polo field were later abandoned and it remained solely a golf club. Glendower has always had an exclusive image and at one stage was referred to as the 'Millionaires' Club'. Financial hardship in the 1970s, however, forced the club to sell off land which had been reserved for a second course.

A variety of trees line the par-four opening hole of this parkland course.

The 7th hole, one of the strongest par-fours at Glendower, is played downhill to a raised green.

SOUTH AFRICAN OPEN WINNERS

1989	Fred Wadsworth (278)
1993	Clinton Whitelaw (279)

SOUTH AFRICAN AMATEUR WINNER

1987	Ben Fouchee

SOUTH AFRICAN STROKE PLAY WINNER

1987	Ben Fouchee (211 over 54 holes)

The club has consistently produced top golfers over the years, one of the most famous being Gavin Levenson, a former South African Open champion and Springbok, who has lived in the vicinity of the club for most of his life.

Within two years of opening, Glendower hosted the Transvaal Open which saw one of Bobby Locke's most remarkable performances ever. The 21-year-old Locke had rounds of 66-69-66-64 for a total of 265, which was the world's lowest winning score at the time. This was only a year after he turned professional and even Locke described his own putting on the last day as phenomenal. He finished 26 shots ahead of the runners-up, Sid Brews and A.T. Tomsett.

When the Transvaal Open returned to Glendower in 1950 it was once again Locke who cruised to victory by 10 shots, although this time with a more moderate total of 280. Locke thrived at Glendower and rated the course very highly. During an exhibition match against Sam Snead which was held there in 1947, he went round the course in 63.

One stunning hole follows another at Glendower Golf Club. The 'character' holes start with the 507-metre, par-five 2nd. Locke rated this hole among his best 18 holes in the world, of which only five were in South Africa. From a picturesque tee one drives across a dam to a narrow fairway flanked by tall trees. A stream runs to the left of the fairway and the wise golfer keeps to the right. Recently, a water hole was positioned to the left of the green, introducing an element of danger for the big hitter attempting to reach the green in two shots. This water is drawn from the dam which features on the short 3rd hole and makes for another intimidating tee shot. Depending on where the tee markers have been placed, it is a medium- to long-iron shot with the water ready to swallow anything that falls to the left.

The dam bordering the 10th green is home to a variety of waterbirds, protected within the nature reserve.

The 4th and 5th holes are good par-fours. Water once more presents itself as a hazard from the 6th to the 9th holes. The short 6th green is fronted by ponds and is followed by a superb golf hole, the 7th, which is a long par-four, downhill all the way to a raised green. A stream has to be carried with the second shot. This is a tranquil part of the course, overhung with large trees, and it brings one back to the dam which adjoins the short 3rd hole.

The 8th hole is another par-five, and it takes a bold golfer to go for the green in two because of the ponds positioned in front of it. The 9th hole is a short par-four but a new water hazard, built for the South African Open when it was played as the 18th, presents problems near the green.

The back nine commences with a strong par-four. It requires two long shots to reach the green which has recently been redesigned to dramatic effect, making this one of the feature holes of the course. A large dam has been extended to the left edge of the green, shored up by railway sleepers in much the same way that renowned American architect Pete Dye left his signature on many water holes around the world.

This same dam has to be carried off the tee at the par-four 11th, and the emphasis on the rest of the second nine is on accuracy rather than length.

The 12th is a fine dogleg with a stream guarding the left side of the fairway. It challenges the player to see how much can be cut off with the tee shot. The stream is also a hazard along the left side of the 13th hole, after which the course turns for home.

The 14th hole appears to be a reasonably easy par-three, but it has a deceptive, sloping green. The 15th hole is a straightforward par-five, as is the par-four 16th. Both, however, have well-bunkered greens. The par-three 17th, measuring 195 metres, requires a long-iron, and the 18th hole travels uphill towards the clubhouse.

Some idea of Glendower's natural beauty can be gathered from its proclamation in 1973 as a nature reserve, to protect the abundant bird life associated with the course. There is a stream running through the middle of the course, linking three dams which attract a prolific number of waterbirds.

GOLDFIELDS WEST GOLF CLUB

Designed by Robert Grimsdell

Some of South Africa's most attractive golf courses are found in unlikely places – the Northern Transvaal bushveld, the arid semi-desert of the northern Cape and, in the case of Goldfields West, concealed behind the mine dumps of the West Rand.

Situated near the gold-mining town of Carletonville, the course has been built in a nature reserve between the mine dumps and a low range of hills. The surrounding countryside may appear desolate and uninteresting, but it provides an abundant water supply and the result is a lush course set in a beautiful, bushy valley. The course is owned by the Driefontein Consolidated Gold Mine.

The club and the course were established in 1947, on the historic farm Driefontein. The first clubhouse, which served until the present building was constructed in 1969, was converted from the original farmhouse. Towards the end of the 19th century this farmhouse had been used as a supply depot and staging post between Johannesburg and Potchefstroom. Ruts of the old stagecoach road can still be seen crossing some of the fairways, although they are now covered by grass.

Robert Grimsdell has been very subtle with the design of the Goldfields West course, and this was a period in his life when he did some of his best work. After 20 years with the Royal Johannesburg Golf club, he resigned his position as club professional in 1946 to concentrate on his main love, which was golf course architecture.

Playing the course is more than just a round of golf – it is a delightful stroll in a relaxing, unspoiled

A variety of wildlife can be seen on the course at Goldfields West.

environment. The variety of wildlife is a special feature of this golf club; herds of buck roam the course, often galloping across the fairways in front of you, and monkeys play in the trees. Flocks of waterbirds inhabit the dams on the course.

Goldfields West is to all outward appearances a gentle round of golf. It has a strong starting stretch and an equally fierce finishing hole, but for the most part it is not a particularly taxing layout. The fairways are generously wide in most cases and the greens are reasonably large and receptive.

Only two par-fours exceed 375 metres; the five par-fives are short by modern standards and are all approximately the same length. However, you do have to plot your tee shots carefully, placing them in the right areas to give yourself a chance of aiming for the flag, and there are some well-placed fairway bunkers to avoid.

There is a high price to pay for missing the greens, because recovery pitches and chips tend to be awkward. The greens themselves have an unusual nap (grain) which makes it difficult to read the lines of putts.

Transvaal greens in earlier times were famous for their nap and the unbelievable way in which putts would break. The nap could be so strong that it was not unusual to see a putt break uphill. Many clubs and golfers considered nap a curse (although Bobby Locke became one of the best putters in the world on these surfaces), and Sid Brews introduced his own strain of grass, Brewsia, at Houghton, which helped to eliminate it partially.

But it was the introduction of bent-grass greens to South Africa which saw nap disappear forever at most courses. Goldfields West has always resisted planting bent grass, preferring their greens which give the course a particular identity and make it difficult to attain low scores.

Conditioning is an important measure of a well-kept course, and Goldfields West is beautifully maintained, with the fine grass growing on the tees almost good enough to putt on.

Goldfields West opens with a relatively short par-four, which is followed by three of the most testing holes on the course in terms of length. The 2nd has possibly the widest fairway on the course, but at 425 metres it requires two powerful shots to reach a green which is bunkered in the front. The 3rd is slightly uphill, returning in the direction of

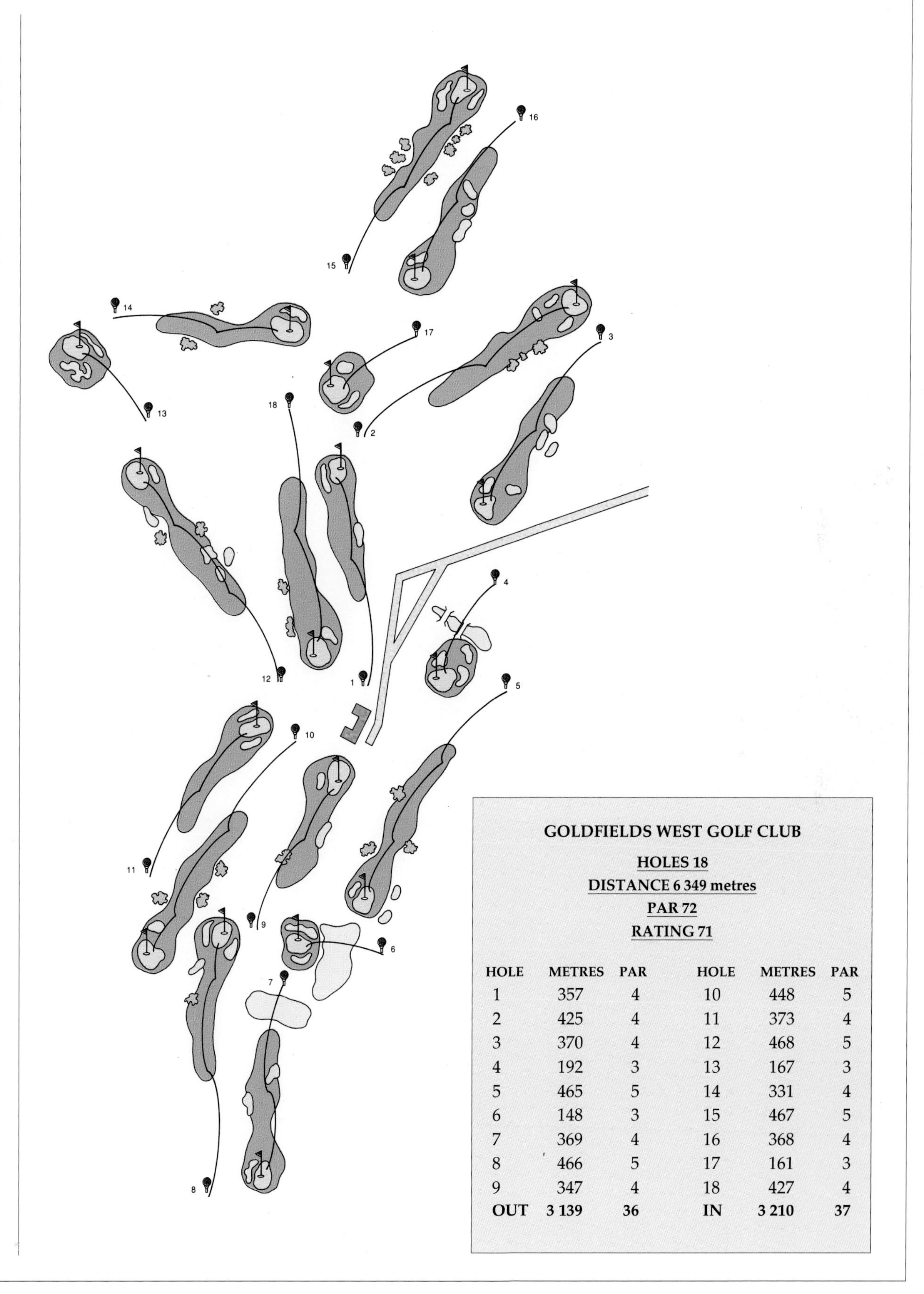

GOLDFIELDS WEST GOLF CLUB

HOLES 18
DISTANCE 6 349 metres
PAR 72
RATING 71

HOLE	METRES	PAR	HOLE	METRES	PAR
1	357	4	10	448	5
2	425	4	11	373	4
3	370	4	12	468	5
4	192	3	13	167	3
5	465	5	14	331	4
6	148	3	15	467	5
7	369	4	16	368	4
8	466	5	17	161	3
9	347	4	18	427	4
OUT	**3 139**	**36**	**IN**	**3 210**	**37**

the clubhouse. A stream crosses the front of the fairway and continues up the right-hand side. These two holes are strokes one and three respectively on the card, and there is a long interval before stroke two at the 18th.

Having already dealt with two difficult approach shots, another long iron is needed for the par-three 4th hole, measuring 192 metres. After this the holes get easier, although the bushy vegetation makes for narrower fairways.

The 5th is an attractive par-five played through an avenue of trees, where work has recently been carried out redesigning the green and improving the drainage. The 6th is a picturesque short hole, hitting from an elevated tee over a dam to a tricky, sloping green which is bunkered on both sides. The 7th is a slight dogleg par-four, winding its way uphill. At the par-five 8th, which returns downhill, a well-struck tee shot offers the possibility of reaching the green in two. The 9th is a fairly straightforward hole, and the 10th and 11th are played up and then down the side of a hill.

The par-five 12th is a straight hole, while the short 13th is played from an elevated tee to a raised green. The 14th is a short but interesting par-four, the green slightly hidden behind bush lining the left side of the fairway. The tee shot has to be kept to the right for the best possible approach to the pin. The par-five 15th requires either a lay-up shot off the tee or the ability to shape the ball from left to right, as there is a narrow stretch of fairway to negotiate in the driving area.

A twisting fairway with bunkers provides complications on the par-four 16th, while the 17th is an undemanding short hole. The 18th, a par-four measuring 427 metres, is a daunting closing hole. A long tee shot is essential to have any chance of reaching the green in two.

Goldfields West regularly plays host to the Western Transvaal Open, one of the major amateur championships in the Transvaal, and was at one time its permanent home. A special atmosphere is always evident at tournaments held here, and many of the country's leading players have enjoyed success on this course.

OPPOSITE: *The 4th hole, with its well-bunkered green bordering a large dam, is one of the more challenging holes on this course.*

A large dam has to be carried to reach the green on the 6th hole.

An imposing water hazard is a feature of the 7th fairway.

HANS MERENSKY GOLF CLUB

Designed by Robert Grimsdell

Lightning is generally regarded as a legitimate reason for suspending play during a round of golf, but at the Hans Merensky Golf Club in Phalaborwa in the north-eastern Transvaal, a buffalo grazing on a fairway has been sufficient reason for players to head back to the clubhouse.

Encounters with wild animals are accepted as one of the hazards for members at this wonderfully different course bordering the Kruger National Park. The 18 holes are fenced off from the Park but this does not deter the animals, who enter through the club's private reserve to the south of the course. Although lions occasionally roam the fairways, the buffalo is regarded as one of the most dangerous animals to encounter because of its unpredictability. It will attack without provocation and has been responsible for more human deaths in the Kruger National Park than any other animal.

During a round of golf at Hans Merensky Golf Club, the conversation inevitably centres around the wildlife on the course. There are plentiful buck and baboons to be seen, warthogs are not uncommon, digging up the fairways to the annoyance of the members, and a herd of hippos can be seen frolicking in the water hole at the 17th. Spotting something more exotic and dangerous like a lion or an elephant is a special moment and a certain degree of wariness must be adopted in their presence, as they do not take kindly to receiving a stinging shot from a golf ball.

The clubhouse, overlooking the 9th green, is one of the largest buildings under thatch in Africa.

A group of members once came across a buffalo grazing on the fairway of the 16th hole and returned to the clubhouse to inform the security officer, Mr Frik Schutte, that this was one obstruction they did not care to interfere with. He thought they were being a bit cowardly and drove to the 16th hole, intending to make the intruder move on. About half-an-hour later he returned to the clubhouse ashen-faced: the buffalo had resented his presence and charged his pick-up, causing severe damage. Not prepared to argue with an aggressive buffalo, the security officer had jumped out and run for the safety of the clubhouse.

The fact that the course abounds with so much wildlife may focus attention away from the layout itself, but it is a course worthy of notice. The late architect, Robert Grimsdell, designed 18 classic holes on this land which used to belong to the National Parks Board. Alterations have been made in recent years but the course has stood the test of time remarkably well.

The Hans Merensky Club is owned by the Palabora Mining Company, which operates the largest opencast copper mine in the world, and in true South African mining tradition it is a club of remarkably high standards. The magnificent clubhouse is one of the largest buildings under thatch in Africa. In addition to golf, the club offers a variety of other sports.

It is named after the late Dr Hans Merensky, one of South Africa's foremost geologists. In 1912 he carried out a geological survey of the rocky Loolekop outcrop that was later to become known as the 'hill of copper'. That outcrop, first mined in the early 1960s, has vanished to become a vast opencast mine. It is now a deep pit almost two kilometres in length and 1,6 kilometres wide.

Construction of the Hans Merensky golf course began in 1966 on land which used to form part of the Kruger National Park. That year the South African House of Assembly approved a trading of land between the Palabora Mining Company and the National Parks Board.

Preparing the site was a massive task as the holes had to be carved out of rugged bushveld, and the planting of Retief grass on the fairways and Florida grass on the greens was all done by hand. Before work could begin, beaters had to drive the animals out of the area and fences were erected to keep them from returning. Even so, workers were constantly confronted by angry elephants or stalking cats and often had to flee to safety.

There have been nine recorded 'kills' on the course (none of which involved people), the most dramatic of which occurred in full view of a women's four-ball about to tee off at the 15th hole. A leopard killed an impala in front of them and dragged it to the upper branches of a tree next to the tee. The scratch marks left on the tree are still clearly visible.

The club hosted the Rothmans Interprovincial in 1974, but it became nationally famous during the 1980s with the televised staging of the Palabora Classic, which was part of the Sunshine Tour agenda. Although this tournament, which unfortunately is no longer contested, was played in the middle of summer when the heat is at its most oppressive, it proved one of the most popular tournaments among the professionals.

The coveted Palabora Classic winner's trophy was a unique work of art – an elephant's head sculptured out of tamboti wood with ivory tusks (fashioned from warthog tusks), set on a central column of red ivory wood and a leadwood base. The elephant's head is modelled on that of Joao, the last surviving member of the Kruger National Park's 'Magnificent Seven' elephants.

Like so many bushveld courses, magnificent trees are features on several holes. There were many hundreds more, but they were flattened by elephants and some of these animals had to be culled to prevent further habitat destruction.

The undulating terrain provides a surprising variety of holes at Hans Merensky. Very few of them are flat and several approach shots have to be played either uphill or downhill. The tricky greens are exceptionally well bunkered.

An attractive feature is that the two starting holes, the 1st and the 10th, are both downhill par-fours, which is an encouraging way to begin a round. What goes down must eventually come up, however, and the 9th and the 18th are punishing uphill par-fours. The short holes are features of the course, and two of them, the 17th and the 8th, are rated among the toughest that the professionals come up against during the Sunshine Tour.

HANS MERENSKY GOLF CLUB

HOLES 18
DISTANCE 6127 metres
PAR 72
RATING 72

HOLE	METRES	PAR	HOLE	METRES	PAR
1	358	4	10	366	4
2	144	3	11	493	5
3	350	4	12	370	4
4	504	5	13	172	3
5	455	5	14	332	4
6	402	4	15	346	4
7	325	4	16	485	5
8	155	3	17	173	3
9	349	4	18	348	4
OUT	**3 042**	**36**	**IN**	**3 085**	**36**

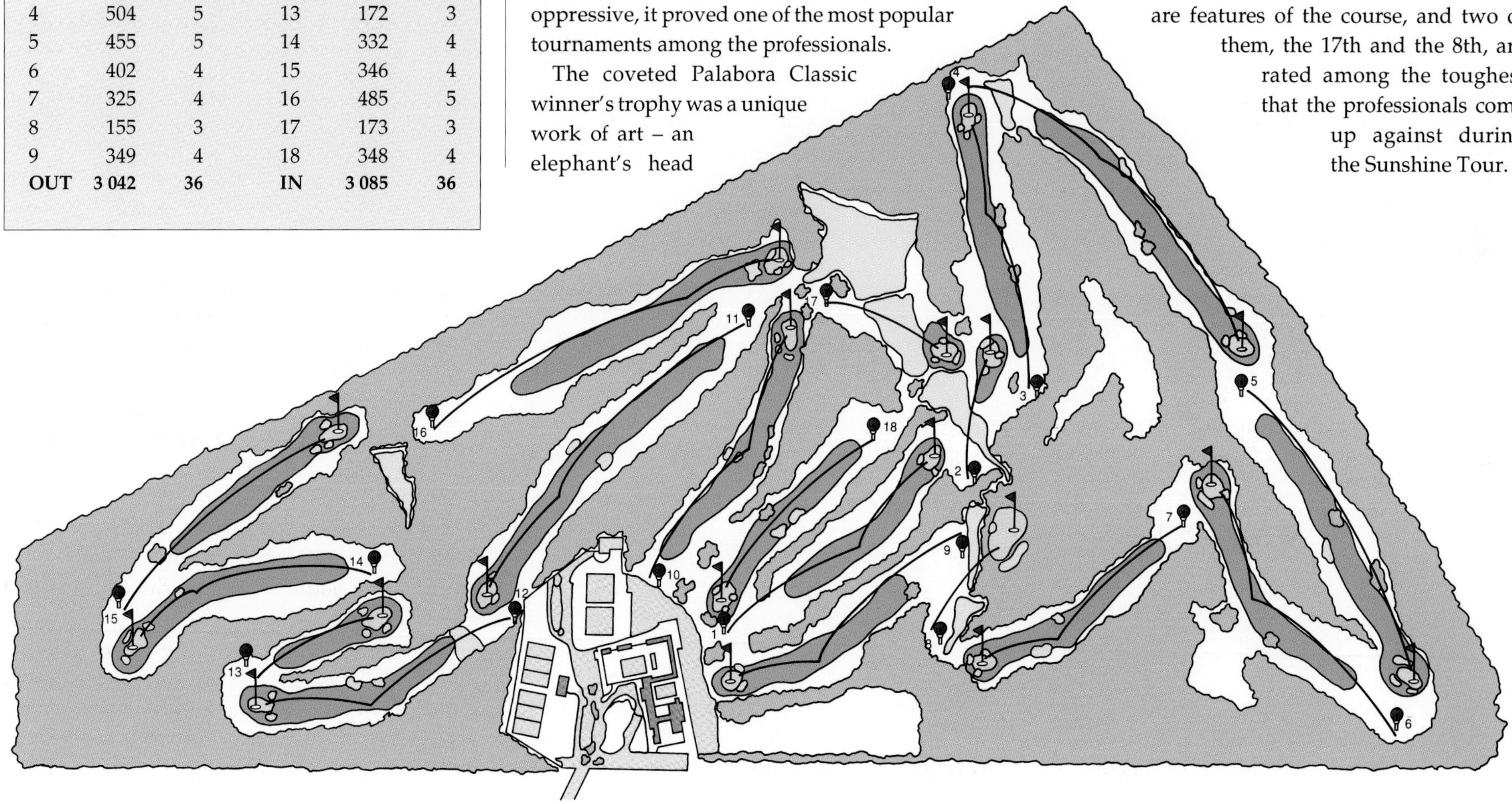

The huge water hole at the 17th is home to a herd of hippos and a crocodile. During the Palabora Classic a few years ago, the hippos were moving from their water hole to a bigger dam to the south of the course when they encountered a three-ball of professionals at the 3rd hole. They grunted and looked aggressive, and the professionals turned tail and fled. One of them, an American, telephoned home that night to say that he had been charged by an angry 'rhino'. The next day the national newspapers in the United States promenaded this story across their front pages, leaving their readers with a vivid description of what it must be like to play golf in 'darkest Africa'.

ABOVE: *The 17th green is precariously situated between an enormous water hole and large, treacherous bunkers.*

OPPOSITE: *A sign warns of the dangers of playing too close to the water near the 18th tee.*

18
PAR 4
STROKE 4
358 M
BEWARE OF

Hippos wallow in the water hazard fronting the 17th green. This spectacular sight has became internationally famous through media coverage.

In the early days of the course the nines were played the other way round, but it became obvious after some years that they had to be swopped to provide a tougher and more spectacular finish.

Off the club tees it is not a particularly long course, with no strikingly tough par-fours, but it pays to be accurate. Stroke one is the 402-metre 6th, a dogleg-right with a large mopane tree blocking the short route to the green. The tee shot has to be kept to the left-hand side of the fairway in order to open up the green.

The tee shot at the 173-metre 17th hole requires a long carry over water to reach the green and can be intimidating for players with higher handicaps. But the hole which really bothers the better golfers, including professionals, is the par-three 8th. This is a relatively new hole – the old 8th having been regarded as one of the easiest on the course. It looks innocuous at first glance, being shorter than the 17th hole at 155 metres, but play it and you become conscious of its myriad challenges. A water hole borders the front and left side of the two-tiered green, which slopes towards the water, and a big bunker guards the right-hand side, while behind the green lies thick bush. During the 1990/91 Sunshine Tour the 8th and the 17th were jointly regarded as the most difficult par-threes, playing to an average score of 3,3.

An outstanding par-four is the 370-metre 12th, where the tee shot must be played to an uphill fairway which is guarded on the right by two large bunkers. Once you have successfully avoided them, you are still left with a difficult approach to a green that slopes steeply from back to front.

The par-fives at Hans Merensky are exceptionally strong holes and have been designed as genuine three-shotters. They certainly do not give any breathing space or the easy prospect of a birdie four. Two of these par-fives, the 4th and 5th, follow each other on the front nine.

PALABORA CLASSIC WINNERS

1985	Mark McNulty (275)*
1986	Fulton Allem (270)
1987	Fulton Allem (271)
1988	Fulton Allem (277)
1989	Stuart Smith (274)**
1990	Tony Johnstone (274)
1991	John Bland (278)

* Won play-off against Hugh Baiocchi
** Won play-off against Ian Palmer

The 4th measures 504 metres, moving gently uphill all the way to a well-bunkered green. It takes two long shots to reach it in two and was adjudged the toughest par-five on the Sunshine Tour during 1990/91, playing to an average of 5,12.

The 5th is 50 metres shorter and a potential birdie hole. However, the green is shallow and bunkers guard the front and the back, catching any long second shot that is not precisely on target.

The par-five 16th is one of the feature holes at Hans Merensky, measuring 485 metres. The fence bordering the Kruger National Park is on the left-hand side of the fairway and animals rustle in the foliage just metres away from the tee. The tee shot is a blind one over a rise from which the fairway drops steeply to the green. For the longer hitters it would be easy to reach in two but for a water hazard situated in front of the green.

The first Palabora Classic was played in 1985 and was won by Mark McNulty after a five-hole play-off against Hugh Baiocchi. McNulty set a course record of nine-under-par 63 in the opening round which remains the lowest score ever achieved at Hans Merensky. The course has undergone several changes since then, however, so it no longer constitutes a record.

Winter is possibly the best time to play golf in Phalaborwa, when the course is lush and green and the weather is usually idyllic. It is also a good time of year to visit the Kruger National Park, and Phalaborwa is close to some of South Africa's most magnificent scenery, including the forests and dams of Tzaneen and Magoebaskloof, and the splendour of the Eastern Transvaal.

OPPOSITE: *The 16th green has to be approached accurately to avoid the perilous sand traps and the water hazard fronting it.*

16

HOUGHTON GOLF CLUB

Designed by A.M. Copland

The beginnings of Houghton can be traced back to the turn of the century when the Johannesburg Golf Club had its course on the slopes of Houghton Ridge, now known as 'The Wilds'.

Prior to the First World War the club split into two groups, with one moving to what is now the nearby Royal Johannesburg and the other establishing the Houghton Estate Golf Club on land adjacent to the present course. This land was leased from the Johannesburg Consolidated Investment Company from 1913 to 1922, when the JCI decided to develop Houghton Estate for housing. They offered the club sufficient ground to build a new course within the township and, as a result, 1923 saw the opening of Houghton Golf Club. The original 18 holes were planned and laid out by the club's first professional, A.M. Copland, on what was previously a bluegum plantation.

For many of the older golfers, Houghton Golf Club will always be associated with the late Sid Brews, who was the club professional for 35 years, from 1935 onwards. Brews was not only a great player, winning eight South African Open titles between 1925 and 1952, but he was a club man of the old professional school and centred his life around the activities at Houghton.

Brews made several significant changes to the course during his years there. He even introduced his own strain of grass, Brewsia, for the Houghton greens, to counter the strong nap which plagued all Transvaal courses. The Brewsia greens lasted from 1939 to 1954, when they were replaced with Florida grass, then later with bent grass.

Although born in England, Brews was always seen to be a South African, leading the way overseas during the 1920s and '30s for Bobby Locke and Gary Player to follow. He won tournaments in Europe and America and was runner-up in the 1934 British Open. Brews died soon after retiring from the club in 1970 at the age of 71. His name is enshrined on a memorial at the club.

Houghton Golf Club has never been shy to take the initiative, and in 1948 it was the first golf club in the Transvaal to introduce a water reticulation system. Other clubs soon followed suit.

Looking back down the tree-lined fairway from the green of the 4th hole, one of Houghton's most challenging par-fours.

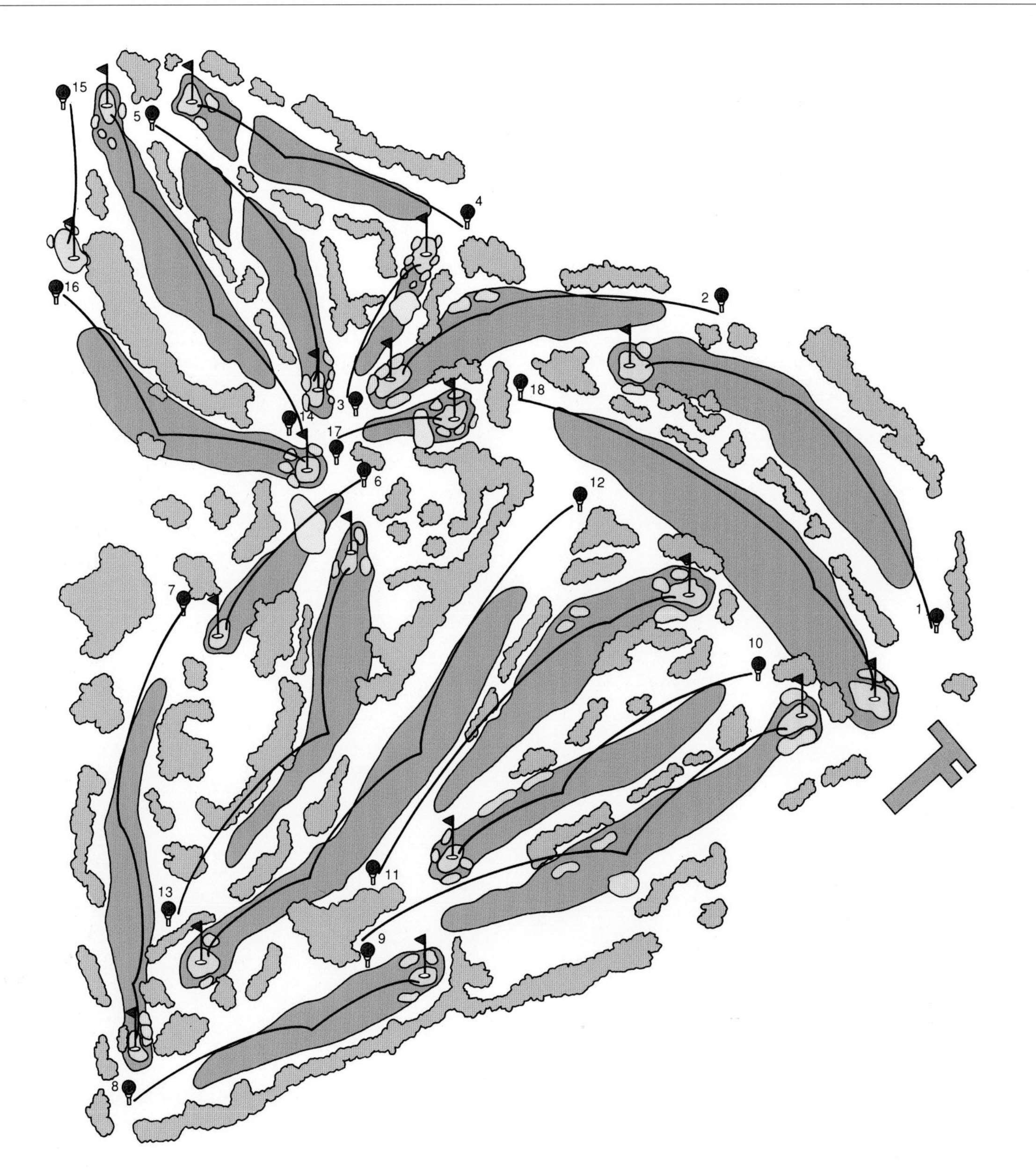

HOUGHTON GOLF CLUB

HOLES 18
DISTANCE 6 434 metres
PAR 72
RATING 71

HOLE	METRES	PAR	HOLE	METRES	PAR
1	392	4	10	337	4
2	368	4	11	367	4
3	138	3	12	532	5
4	410	4	13	390	4
5	415	4	14	463	5
6	199	3	15	172	3
7	461	5	16	371	4
8	373	4	17	141	3
9	480	5	18	425	4
OUT	**3 236**	**36**	**IN**	**3 198**	**36**

Only becoming fashionable as a national championship course after the Second World War, Houghton has been host to eight South African Opens, including the 1992 Open.

The first national championships to be held at Houghton were the Amateur and the Open in 1951. This saw the extraordinary feat of four home-club members reaching the semi-finals of the Amateur, which had never been done before or been equalled since. Teddy Irwin, who was a remarkable character and a wonderful humorist, beat Mickey Janks in the final. The defeated semi-finalists were Jack Gorley, who later became president of the Transvaal Golf Union, and Bobby Faivelson.

Janks, adding to the South African Open crown he won at East London in 1948, triumphed in the Amateur at Humewood in 1952. That was to prove another proud year for Houghton Golf Club, with three members holding all three of the country's major trophies. Janks won the Amateur trophy, Brews the Open, and Reggie Green the South African women's crown. This is a feat unparalleled in the history of club golf in southern Africa.

Gary Player, whose early dabbling in golf course architecture was with Sid Brews, carried out some alterations in the early 1970s to hone the Houghton course to modern tournament standards. He obviously did a good job because the 1976 Open at Houghton produced one of the highest winning scores of the last 30 years – the 287 posted by Dale Hayes and John Fourie. Hayes went on to win his only Open title in an 18-hole play-off.

The course covers a compact triangular area and is not particularly extensive, but the ground has been well utilized, with tall, stately trees lining each hole. It has proved a difficult layout and has seen some memorable duels over the years.

Gary Player took on the tempestuous Tommy Bolt at Houghton Golf Club during their exhibition series in 1959, where the gallery was treated to some blatant gamesmanship by Bolt, who was at that time the reigning United States Open champion. Whenever Bolt was a hole down he sulked and wanted to concede the match, only continuing after Player pleaded with him to do so. Bolt's tactics succeeded and he won the match at the 18th hole. Houghton was also the Johannesburg venue for Player's matches against Arnold Palmer in 1962, and Jack Nicklaus in 1966.

When the South African Open returned to Houghton in 1992, competitors found several changes had been made to the course since the previous Open in 1984. An unusual feature of Houghton had been its three par-fives, three par-threes and 12 par-fours. It now has the conventional four par-fives and four par-threes.

The club sold off a piece of ground at the far end of the course from the clubhouse, which included

The fairway and green of the par-four 16th hole.

The green of the par-three 17th hole, looking back across the water to the tee.

SOUTH AFRICAN OPEN WINNERS

1951	Bobby Locke (277)
1962	Harold Henning (285)
1966	Gary Player (278)
1968	Gary Player (274)
1976	Dale Hayes (287)*
1979	Gary Player (279)
1984	Tony Johnstone (274)
1992	Ernie Els (273)

* Won play-off against John Fourie

SOUTH AFRICAN AMATEUR WINNERS

1951	Teddy Irwin
1962	John Hayes
1973	Andries Oosthuizen

SOUTH AFRICAN STROKE PLAY WINNERS

1973	George Harvey (281)*

* Won play-off against Andries Oosthuizen

the entire par-four 15th hole as well as the teeing ground of the 16th. The new 15th is a par-three, and the shape of the par-four 16th has been changed. In order to maintain a par of 72, the 9th hole has been redesigned and lengthened into a par-five.

With the exception of the par-five 12th, which at 532 metres is one of the longest par-fives in the country, Houghton is not particularly long by modern championship standards. Two of the short holes come early in the round: the 138-metre 3rd hole which requires just a short iron over water, and the mighty 199-metre 6th hole, where once more water must be carried, but this time with a much longer club. The next eight holes are either par-fours or par-fives, before reaching the 15th.

The short 17th often plays a decisive role in tournaments at Houghton. It is played slightly uphill which makes for a deceptive choice of club. The green slopes towards a water hazard.

The 18th is an outstanding finishing hole, winding 425 metres uphill to the clubhouse. There was a dramatic finish here in the 1979 Open when Englishman Ian Mosey missed a short putt on the final day to give the title to Gary Player. Player has a wonderful record at Houghton, having won the Open there three times, and the South African PGA and the Dunlop Masters twice each.

OPPOSITE: *This attractive water hole presents a hazard short of the green on the 3rd hole.*

MACCAUVLEI GOLF CLUB

Designed by Colonel S.V. Hotchkin and George Peck

For some unknown reason there is a general dearth of bunkers on many of the older South African golf courses, unlike those found in the British Isles or the United States. But at Maccauvlei Golf Club, which is situated on the outskirts of Vereeniging in the Transvaal, one finds a plentiful supply of large sand traps as well as a number of water hazards, which make this picturesque, tree-lined course on the banks of the Vaal River a most challenging round of golf.

Maccauvlei (literally Muscovy duck marsh) is not one of the better known courses to the new generation of golfers in South Africa. However, it has an excellent pedigree which dates back to its development in 1926 when Louis and Teddy Marks, the directors of Vereeniging Estates, conceived the idea of establishing a championship golf course on this site which lies across the Vaal River from Vereeniging. On its completion, Maccauvlei golf course was immediately considered to be of championship status.

When the South African championships were first staged at the course in 1927, it was considered one of the best layouts in the country, as a report of

Bunkers and a large water hazard lie in wait for any misplaced shots to the 2nd green.

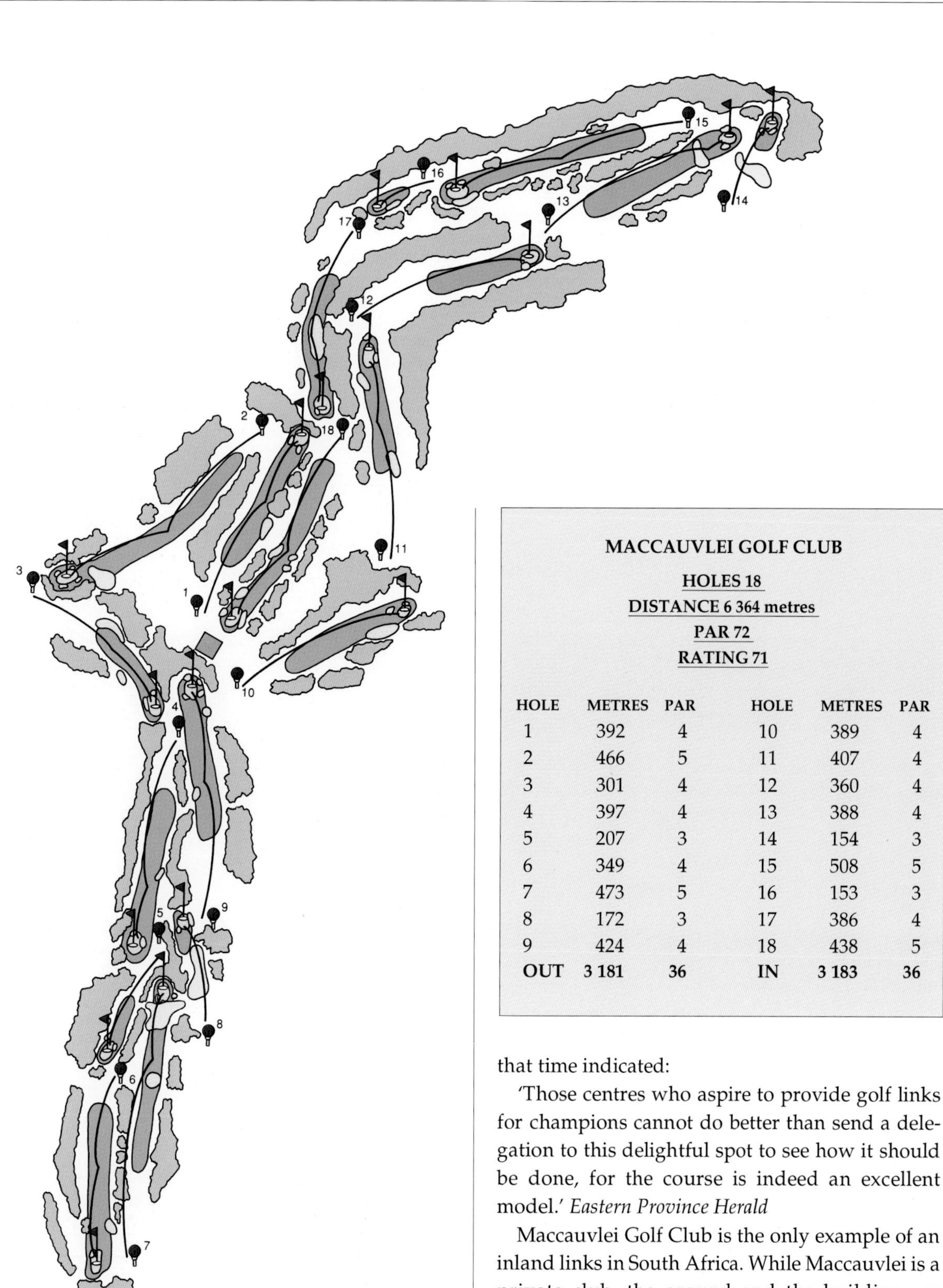

MACCAUVLEI GOLF CLUB

HOLES 18
DISTANCE 6 364 metres
PAR 72
RATING 71

HOLE	METRES	PAR	HOLE	METRES	PAR
1	392	4	10	389	4
2	466	5	11	407	4
3	301	4	12	360	4
4	397	4	13	388	4
5	207	3	14	154	3
6	349	4	15	508	5
7	473	5	16	153	3
8	172	3	17	386	4
9	424	4	18	438	5
OUT	**3 181**	**36**	**IN**	**3 183**	**36**

that time indicated:

'Those centres who aspire to provide golf links for champions cannot do better than send a delegation to this delightful spot to see how it should be done, for the course is indeed an excellent model.' *Eastern Province Herald*

Maccauvlei Golf Club is the only example of an inland links in South Africa. While Maccauvlei is a private club, the ground and the building are owned by Anglo-American, and the club's patron is Mr Harry Oppenheimer.

The original land was a wilderness of sandy waste, scrub and dunes, ideal terrain for a links. The design of Maccauvlei golf course is credited to Colonel S.V. Hotchkin, one of Britain's leading golf course architects of that era, who is famed for the work he did at the Humewood Golf Club in Port Elizabeth. There is reference, however, to the initial design work at Maccauvlei being executed by George Peck, who constructed the present East London layout.

Although Maccauvlei lies on the Orange Free State side of the Vaal River, the club has always been affiliated to the Southern Transvaal Golf Association. For many years it has held two of the more important tournaments on the Transvaal amateur calendar, the Oppenheimer Trophy and the Vaal Amateur. The winners of these events turn the club's honours board into a virtual who's who of South African golf.

In its heyday, between 1927 and 1949, Maccauvlei hosted four South African Open championships. Three of these were won by Sid Brews, who captured eight Open titles in all. The other went to Bobby Locke in 1938, the year he turned professional. For a while Locke was the professional at Vereeniging Country Club, on the opposite bank of the Vaal River to Maccauvlei Golf Club.

During its early years, before the Second World War, the club was a favourite weekend haunt for the elite of Johannesburg society. They would take the train to Maccauvlei, enjoy five-star hospitality at the club's dormie house and relax on the golf course. Maccauvlei Station, which no longer exists, adjoined the 4th hole and was the first stop outside Vereeniging. It gave rise to the Springbok Radio programme, 'Next Stop Maccauvlei'.

At 6 364 metres the course is relatively short by Highveld standards, but the best 36-hole score obtained during one of the amateur tournaments held at this club is an eight-under-par 136, carded by Brian Jacobs in 1974.

The course begins with a straightforward par-four hole, followed by a curving par-five with water guarding the green. The 3rd hole is a short, uphill par-four of 301 metres, returning to the clubhouse, which is still the original building. Just off the fairway, among a clump of trees, is a tiny cemetery and a memorial to those who died during the Anglo-Boer War. It is near this spot that Boer soldiers ambushed a troop train, and one of those to escape was the young Winston Churchill.

A picturesque bridge links the green of the par-three 14th hole to the tee.

For the remainder of the front nine the holes are reasonably flat. The 5th hole is a fine par-three, and the 9th hole, which travels back towards the clubhouse, at 424 metres is the longest par-four on the course. On the par-three 8th hole, a pond occupies what was once a bunker. Many of the older bunkers have been filled in with soil.

The back nine comprises several diverse holes. The stretch from the 12th to the 17th hole is a particularly tranquil section which winds its way past shady trees and the river bank. These holes require a series of accurate approach shots if the pitfalls are to be avoided. The par-four 13th hole is particularly beautiful, with its undulating fairway and a wooden bridge crossing a stream which flows into a pond near the green.

The dogleg 17th hole boasts the largest bunker in South Africa, comparable to some of the famous wastes of sand at Pine Valley, New Jersey, in the United States. The tee shot should be played short of the bunker, whereupon the golfer is confronted with a semi-blind shot over the distant crest of the bunker to the green. Only the top of the flag is visible from this point. It is not a formidable hole for the low-handicap player, but the vast stretch of

The 14th green: the velvet texture of the bent-grass greens contributes to Maccauvlei's first-class layout status.

SOUTH AFRICAN OPEN WINNERS

1927	Sid Brews (301)
1933	Sid Brews (297)
1938	Bobby Locke (279)
1949	Sid Brews (291)

SOUTH AFRICAN AMATEUR WINNERS

1927	George Chantler
1928	Bernard Wynne

sand does have a psychological effect on one's game. To one side of the bunker is a dead tree bearing the skull of an ox and a board with the inscription 'Last Stop Maccauvlei', which was placed there by the greenkeeper at that time in the same humorous vein as the hangman's noose at Pete Dye's 16th hole at Oak Tree, Oklahoma, in the United States.

Maccauvlei Golf Club has in recent years been resurrected by a vibrant committee and management. It has been suitably upgraded with a new irrigation system and bent-grass greens to attain first-class layout status and the club often hosts championships as part of the popular Winter Tour.

The 9th hole, the longest par-four on the course, returns golfers to the old clubhouse building.

Beyond the 3rd hole, among a clump of trees, lies a small cemetery and memorial for soldiers who died in the Anglo-Boer War.

ROODEPOORT COUNTRY CLUB

Designed by Gary Player, Ron Kirby and Denis Griffiths

Roodepoort Country Club, which was completed in 1985, was the first course designed by Gary Player in the Witwatersrand region. The main feature of this virtually treeless layout, set in country surroundings on the West Rand, is its magnificent greens. Full of contours and slopes, they are considered to be among the best putting surfaces in the country.

Although Player has been involved in the design of many golf courses around the world, the majority of them being in the United States, only in recent years has he designed courses on a regular basis in South Africa. Player designed the Roodepoort course in partnership with American course architects Ron Kirby and Denis Griffiths, who also worked independently of Player in remodelling the Kensington and the Royal Johannesburg West courses during the 1980s. They split up soon after the completion of Roodepoort and Player joined forces with another American, Karl Litten.

The development of Roodepoort Country Club is unique in two respects. It was the first stadium-style course built in South Africa, along similar lines to those which proliferated in the United

Roodepoort Country Club's imposing clubhouse stands on a rise overlooking all 18 holes.

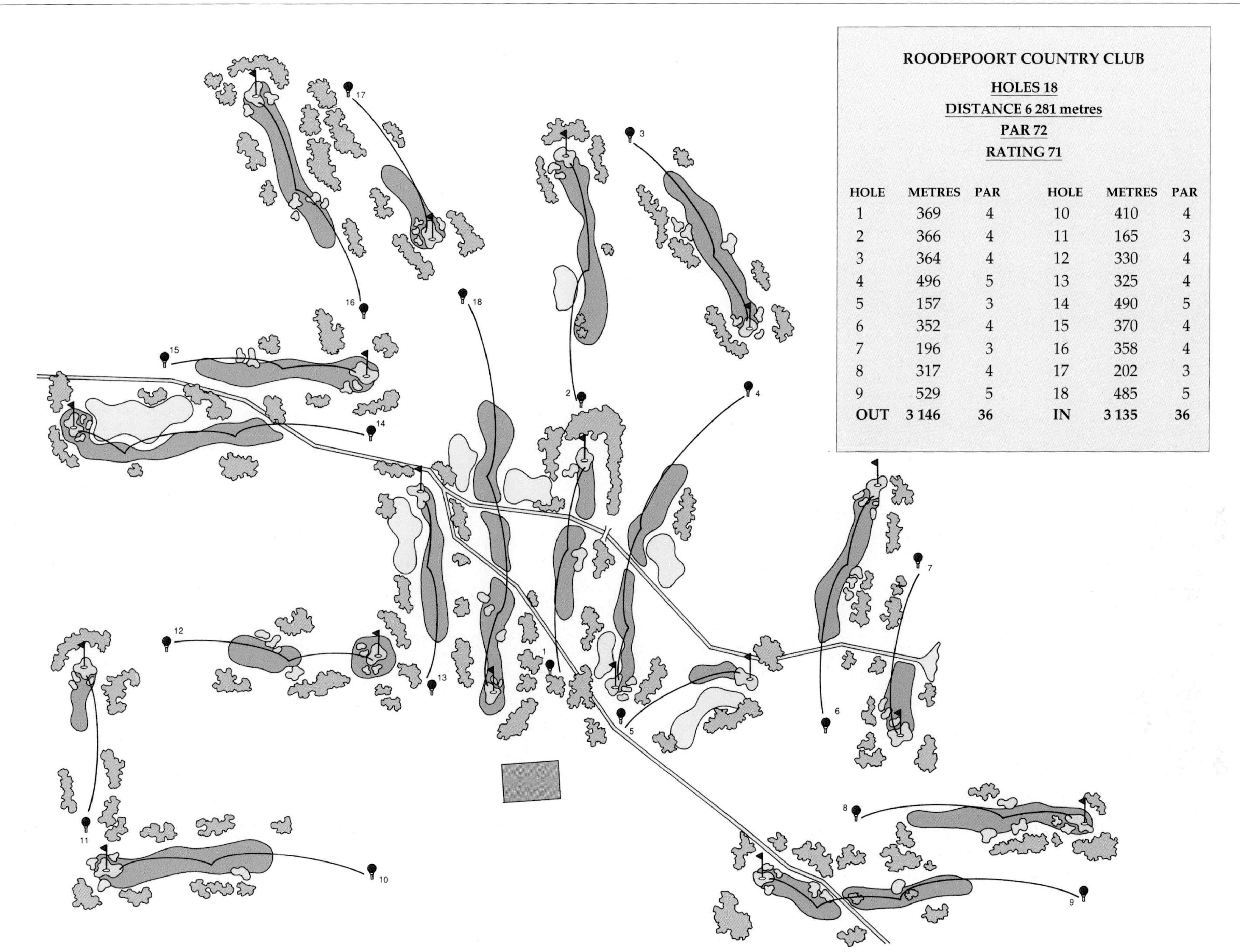

ROODEPOORT COUNTRY CLUB

HOLES 18
DISTANCE 6 281 metres
PAR 72
RATING 71

HOLE	METRES	PAR	HOLE	METRES	PAR
1	369	4	10	410	4
2	366	4	11	165	3
3	364	4	12	330	4
4	496	5	13	325	4
5	157	3	14	490	5
6	352	4	15	370	4
7	196	3	16	358	4
8	317	4	17	202	3
9	529	5	18	485	5
OUT	**3 146**	**36**	**IN**	**3 135**	**36**

States during the 1980s, with natural spectator mounds. In addition, while the club is run as a private club by the committee and the management staff, who are employed by the club, the fixed assets are owned by the Roodepoort City Council. The few municipal courses existing in South Africa are generally of average quality, catering mainly for beginners. However, the Roodepoort City Council went to considerable expense in providing an outstanding facility for golfers on the West Rand, and the Roodepoort Country Club course cost more than R2-million to construct.

The holes are well spaced, as one of the original intentions was to provide an area for housing development within the course boundaries. With no trees to contend with, Roodepoort is wide open, which tends to detract from the strength of the shot-making challenges.

The course has been the venue for the annual South African Skins tournament since 1988. Played in November, when the rough is still thin before the summer rains, long-hitting professionals like South African Open champion Wayne Westner and American John Daly have ridiculed some of the holes. Without any tough penalties for being off-line they were able to drive the shorter par-fours. This is certainly not what Player intended when he designed the course.

The degree of difficulty in playing Roodepoort for the club golfer depends on where the pins are

The par-four opening hole at Roodepoort looks straightforward, but a large, undulating green presents problems.

The 13th green: the contoured, sloping greens on this course are considered to be among the best putting surfaces in the country.

SOUTH AFRICAN SKINS WINNERS	
1988	Gary Player (R93 000)
1989	Gary Player (R100 000)
1990	John Daly (R86 000)
1991	Gary Player (R81 000)
1992	Wayne Westner (R115 000)

positioned. There are some exceptionally tricky areas on the greens, some of which have slopes to rival those at Augusta National, home of the prestigious United States Masters tournament. Well-bunkered fairways and greens present the main hazards, although water also provides problems on several of the holes.

The four par-five holes – the 4th, the 9th, the 14th and the 18th – are possibly the most interesting on the course, challenging in their design, and neither too long nor too short.

The 496-metre 4th hole, which doglegs sharply to the left, is a superb test for any golfer. Starting from a high tee, water is the first hazard to be encountered to the left-hand side of the fairway, making it impossible to bypass the dogleg. The length of the second shot depends on how close to the water the player has dared to place his drive. The second shot then has to deal with a dam which runs along the right-hand side of the fairway to the front edge of the green. The long-hitter trying to get home in two can either fade his second shot to the left of the fairway, attempting to run the ball on to the putting surface, or attempt to carry the water. Both shots are equally daunting. The tiered green is one of the fastest greens on the course and during Skins tournaments it is not unheard of for putts from the back to run right off the green and on to its front fringe.

There are cross bunkers and a drainage sluice to be carried with the second shot to the 529-metre 9th hole which, like the 4th hole, is played slightly downhill. In addition, the fairway narrows in the driving area while the green is set at an extraordinarily steep angle.

The 490-metre 14th hole takes even more courage to hit in two shots than the 4th. There is no real trouble off the tee, but a long, well-placed drive is necessary to have any chance of reaching the green in two shots. A large dam which laps the edge of the fairway, extends about 180 metres all the way to the relatively small green which lies between two rolling mounds.

The final par-five is the 523-metre closing hole and here it pays to be circumspect off the tee as water holes are well within reach on both sides of the fairway. A long drive carrying the water to the right must land on a narrow piece of fairway and also has to contend with the drainage sluice which runs through the course. It takes a powerful shot to carry this one from the back tee. Having found the fairway, numerous bunkers have to be negotiated before arriving at the elevated green. All in all, this is a magnificent finishing hole, laid out in full view of the clubhouse.

Roodepoort Country Club's clubhouse, which dwarfs the more conventional golf clubhouses found elsewhere in Johannesburg, cost more to build than the course itself.

Situated on a rise, the clubhouse overlooks the full 18 holes. Its spectacular size gives the building an imposing 'American' look. While on the course, one never strays too far away from the clubhouse during play and the exposed, treeless nature of the course allows the spectator to follow play from the raised veranda of the clubhouse.

The par-five 18th hole, with its large water hazard in the driving area.

From the 14th fairway, looking over the dam towards the undulating green.

ROYAL JOHANNESBURG GOLF CLUB

Designed by Robert Grimsdell (East) and Laurie Waters (West)

Royal Johannesburg Golf Club, which celebrated its centenary in 1991, and Durban Country Club have for many years been ranked as the two South African golf courses of international distinction. Royal Johannesburg was the first South African club to host an international event, being the venue for the second Commonwealth tournament, held in 1959. With two 18-hole courses, one of them the championship East layout which has been host to seven South African Opens since the Second World War, Royal Johannesburg members have one of the finest golf facilities in the country.

Originally known as Johannesburg Golf Club, in July 1931 King George V granted the club permission to use the prefix 'Royal', making it one of four Royal golf clubs in South Africa.

While the club itself is over 100 years old, the two courses are of more recent vintage. The first course was established in the Hillbrow area, but was moved several times. In 1909, land which is now part of the West course was purchased for £11 000 in the area beyond Orange Grove, by Sir Lionel Phillips and Sir George Farrar and Sir Abe Bailey, two other mining magnates.

Johannesburg Golf Club professional Laurie Waters, who apprenticed under 'Old' Tom Morris at St Andrews in Scotland, was responsible for the

The clubhouse at Royal Johannesburg, overlooking the East course's 18th green.

design of the original West course. Known as the father of South African golf, he introduced the first grass tees and greens to Johannesburg. Members assisted in the construction of the course by dragging heavy railway lines behind teams of oxen to scuffle the ground, which was the principle of fairway preparation and maintenance at that time. Waters won the first South African Open, held in 1903, and was to win the title four times, his last being the first Open held at Royal Johannesburg's West course in 1920.

ROYAL JOHANNESBURG GOLF CLUB

HOLES 36

EAST COURSE			WEST COURSE		
DISTANCE 6 825 metres			DISTANCE 6 113 metres		
PAR 72			PAR 71		
RATING 73			RATING 69		
HOLE	METRES	PAR	HOLE	METRES	PAR
1	473	5	1	360	4
2	228	3	2	391	4
3	418	4	3	399	4
4	444	4	4	338	4
5	145	3	5	104	3
6	530	5	6	344	4
7	384	4	7	445	5
8	489	5	8	188	3
9	366	4	9	464	5
OUT	**3 477**	**37**	**OUT**	**3 033**	**36**
10	469	4	10	382	4
11	467	4	11	380	4
12	186	3	12	165	3
13	359	4	13	410	4
14	398	4	14	178	3
15	199	3	15	389	4
16	448	4	16	427	4
17	354	4	17	311	4
18	468	5	18	438	5
IN	**3 348**	**35**	**IN**	**3 080**	**35**

In 1933, the members felt the need for a second course and, through the generosity of certain members, a portion of land known as Rough's Farm was acquired for this purpose.

The East layout was completed in 1935 and is a lasting monument to Robert Grimsdell, possibly South Africa's finest golf course architect, who was the club professional and greenkeeper at Royal Johannesburg for more than 20 years. A competitive golfer in his youth and a devotee of the famous English golf course architect Harry Colt, Grimsdell came to Royal Johannesburg in 1926.

The two courses were to be known as the 'old' (West) and the 'new' (East), and involved the construction of 21 new holes of which Grimsdell was both architect and builder.

It took Grimsdell three years to complete the East course. He was removed on a stretcher once he had accomplished the task, having fallen ill from nervous exhaustion and an infection brought about by working in the unhygienic swamp out of which the 6th hole was created. The course is laid out in hilly terrain, and was constructed in a period when heavy machinery was practically non-existent, so Grimsdell had to work with oxen to clear 80 acres of gumtrees and wattle.

No sooner were the two courses finished than the decision was made to build a new clubhouse in a position more central to both courses. The building was finally completed in March 1939, and stands proudly overlooking the East course's 18th green.

The East course hosted its first South African Open in 1946, which was won by Bobby Locke. It boasts a proud list of Open champions, with Gary Player, Bobby Cole and David Frost being chief among them. Player has won the Open three times at Royal Johannesburg, in 1972, 1977 and 1981, but possibly the most famous of the Open championships held at Royal Johannesburg was the one Player lost in 1959 to Denis Hutchinson, the last amateur to win the title.

Hutchinson and Player were paired together for the last two rounds on the final day of play, with Player five shots ahead. Although Player was only 23 years old and had not yet won any of his nine major championships, there was confidence in him

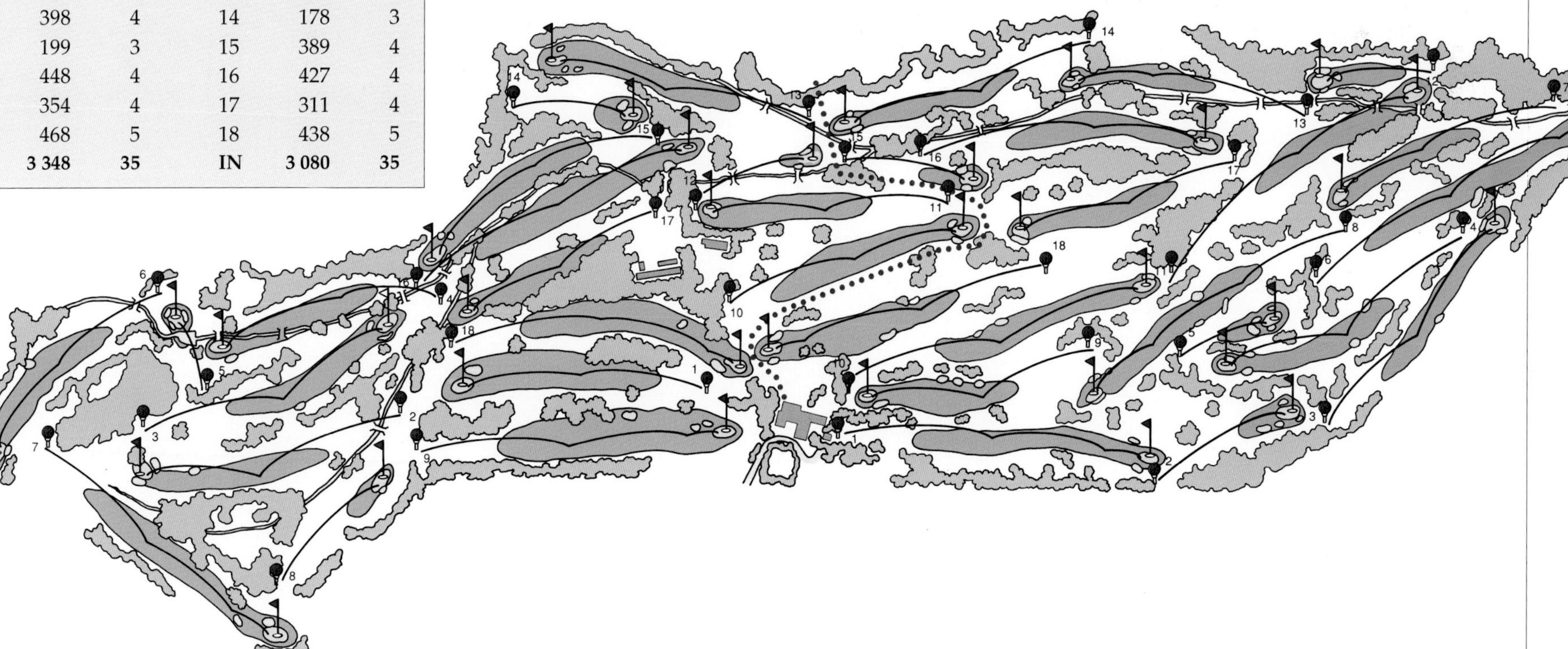

The well-bunkered 5th green on the East course also features an intimidating water hazard.

winning his second South African Open. Player scored 70 in the third round with an eagle at the par-five 18th hole and still led Hutchinson, who had returned a 69, by four shots. The last round was a dramatic one. Hutchinson, who was celebrating his 27th birthday that day, birdied four holes in a row, from the 3rd to the 6th, to level the scores. Hutchinson edged one ahead when Player dropped a shot at the short 12th hole. The young professional bounced back with a birdie-three at the 14th hole and they played level to the final hole, both recovering well under considerable pressure. At the par-five 18th hole both reached the green in two. Hutchinson pushed his first putt six feet wide of the hole after Player had putted up within half that distance, but it was Hutchinson who holed his second putt and Player who missed. It was a well-fought battle, and the gallery flocked around the new champion.

Although the West course has always been overshadowed by the East course as a championship venue, it is nevertheless a beautiful layout with some magnificent holes. Neither as long nor as testing as the East course, it still requires precision golf. The club's annual Silver Vase tournament, a prestigious 36-hole event competed for by invited amateurs on the first Sunday in December, is played over the West and East courses.

Although the ball travels further in the rarefied Highveld air, during the summer months when there is limited run on the fairways the East course may play long, especially when compared to the flattering lengths obtained in the dryness of winter. It is always a gratifying walk, however, through the stretches of tall trees which define the holes.

The East course is not far short of 7 000 metres off the back tees and boasts several fierce holes. The 228-metre 2nd hole is one of the longest par-threes in the country and there are two intimidating par-fours at the start of the back nine – the 10th hole is 469 metres, and the 11th hole, 467 metres. The 11th is an outstanding hole, played from an elevated tee into a valley, with the fairway curving to the right

OPPOSITE: *At 104 metres, the West course's picturesque 5th hole is one of the shortest par-threes in the country.*

A large water hazard hugs the green of the East course's 11th hole.

The 17th green on the East course, surrounded by bunkers and trees.

SOUTH AFRICAN OPEN WINNERS

1904	Laurie Waters (143)
1920	Laurie Waters (302)
1925	Sid Brews (295)
1946	Bobby Locke (285)
1959	Denis Hutchinson (amateur) (282)
1972	Gary Player (274)
1974	Bobby Cole (272)
1977	Gary Player (273)
1981	Gary Player (272)*
1986	David Frost (275)

* Won play-off against John Bland and Warren Humphreys

SOUTH AFRICAN AMATEUR WINNERS

1904	Richard Southey (301)
1920	H. Gordon Stewart (315)

(The South African Amateur was contested over match play from 1925.)

1925	Thomas McLelland
1946	Jimmy Boyd
1959	Arthur Walker
1967	Derek Kemp
1980	Etienne Groenewald
1991	Desvonde Botes

SOUTH AFRICAN STROKE PLAY WINNERS

1980	Etienne Groenewald (293)
1991	Nic Henning (278)

between tall trees. The green is protected in the front by a large water hazard.

The course drops considerably in height from the 1st hole, and the 8th and 17th holes climb steeply back uphill before reaching the finishing holes in front of the clubhouse. The low-lying holes, with a stream flowing between their fairways, are susceptible to flooding after heavy rains.

Royal Johannesburg has been described as a lasting memorial to the work and foresight of a long succession of members devoted to the service of golf. The club has always played a leading role in the development of the game in South Africa; the Transvaal Golf Union was started by the club, as was the Senior Golfers' Society, while the Transvaal Amateur championship and Transvaal Open were also initiated here.

OPPOSITE: *An aerial view of the tree-lined East and West courses showing the hilly terrain and the well-bunkered greens that are characteristic of Royal Johannesburg.*

THE WANDERERS GOLF CLUB

Designed by Robert Grimsdell and Felix Oliver

The Wanderers, in the heart of Johannesburg's exclusive residential belt, has become one of the best-known courses in South Africa as a direct result of the national exposure it has received as permanent host of the annual South African PGA championship. It is fitting that one of the country's premier tournaments should be held on this challenging course, which is owned by one of South Africa's oldest and most prestigious sports clubs.

The foresight of Victor Kent, who served as the first chairman of the Wanderers Golf Club during the period 1939 to 1948, enabled the members of this club to enjoy golf in one of the more exclusive areas of Johannesburg.

The original Wanderers Club was situated in the city of Johannesburg, but Kent realized that in the future land would be needed in the suburbs, as the railways were likely to appropriate the ground on which the club was then situated. Much to the consternation of the committee, who believed he had over-extended the finances of the club, he purchased the property in Illovo on which the present Wanderers complex stands.

Robert Grimsdell was enlisted to design the course with the assistance of the first club captain, Felix Oliver. Initially, nine holes were opened for play, then 12, and finally 18 in 1939.

Leaving the clubhouse, the stroke-two 10th hole plays from an elevated tee through a slight depression, then uphill to the green.

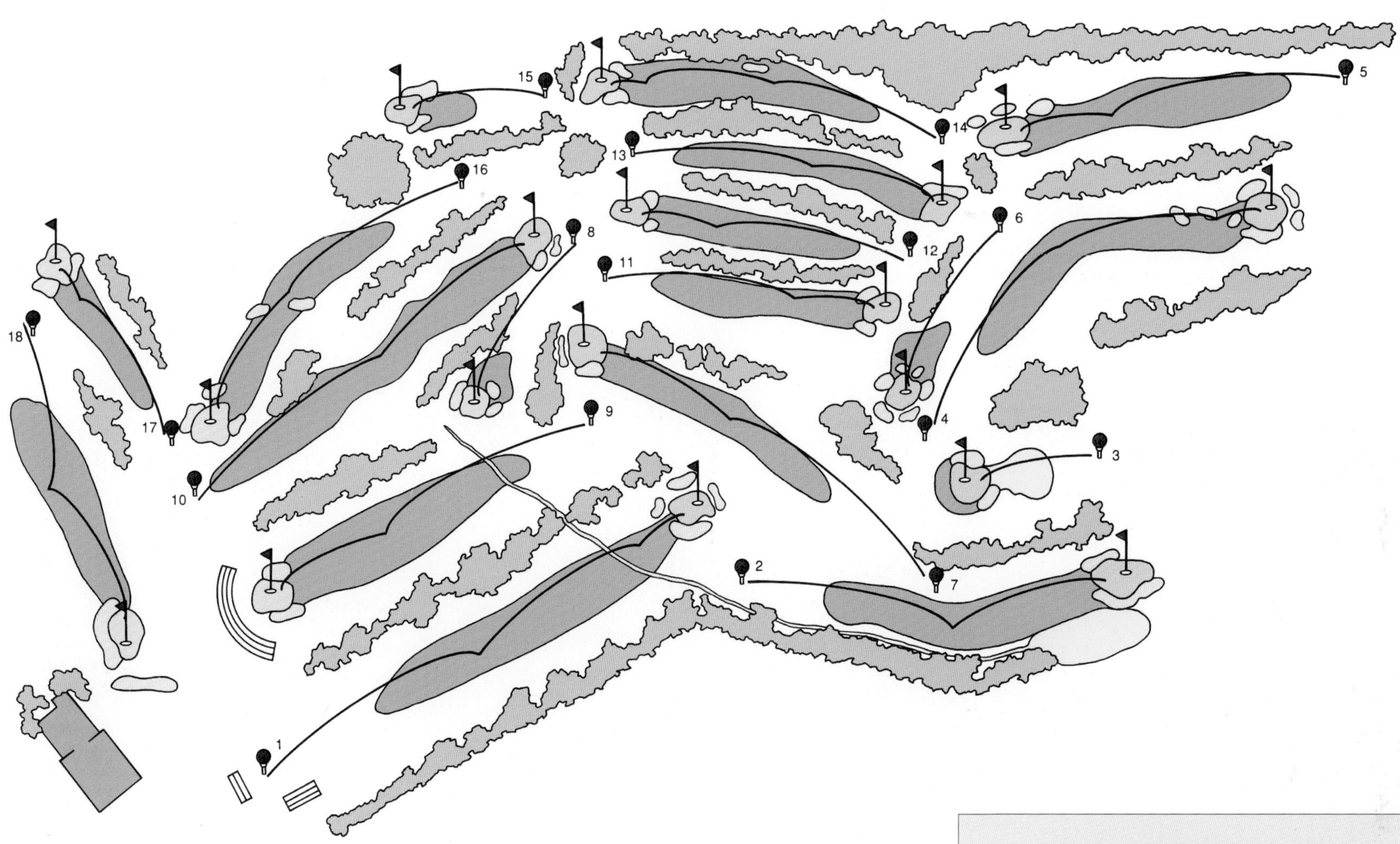

In the 1950s three of the opening holes, the 2nd, 3rd and the 4th – which was generally regarded as one of the most beautiful holes on the course – were demolished to make way for the Wanderers cricket stadium. This was completed in 1956 and today adjoins the par-five 1st hole. Three new holes, the present 4th, 5th and 6th, were opened at the same time. The golf clubhouse and course are separated from the main club buildings and sports fields by Corlett Drive.

The South African PGA championship has been held at Wanderers since 1972. Louis Luyt sponsored the PGA in the early 1970s and there were problems holding it at Huddle Park, a municipal course adjoining Royal Johannesburg Golf Club. In 1971 there was a three-way play-off between Tienie Britz, Englishman Peter Oosterhuis and Don Gammon, which Britz won to retain his title. The play-off had to be held over until the Monday as play was not allowed on Sundays.

Luyt and the PGA then approached Wanderers to act as host in 1972. The committee was reluctant at first as they felt the course was not at its prime during November when the tournament was due to be held. In response to this, Luyt gave the club a R25 000 loan to install a water reticulation system, on the condition that it would stage the PGA championship for five years, and that the loan be paid off from gate money received.

The tournament has never left the club, although Luyt's sponsorship ended in 1976 and Lexington's long tenure as sponsors began in 1977. Next to the

THE WANDERERS GOLF CLUB

HOLES 18
DISTANCE 6 469 metres
PAR 71
RATING 71

HOLE	METRES	PAR	HOLE	METRES	PAR
1	531	5	10	459	4
2	388	4	11	383	4
3	157	3	12	379	4
4	479	5	13	371	4
5	404	4	14	448	5
6	184	3	15	175	3
7	413	4	16	393	4
8	179	3	17	310	4
9	423	4	18	393	4
OUT	**3 158**	**35**	**IN**	**3 311**	**36**

South African Open, the PGA crown is the most coveted title of the Sunshine Tour, and winning it brings an invitation to the World Series of Golf in the United States.

The Wanderers has probably held more professional tournaments than any other club in South Africa. A total of 21 PGA championships have been hosted at this tree-lined course, and the prize money has risen from R25 000 in 1972 to R500 000 in 1993. Prior to this, the Transvaal Open was played there in 1964 and 1970.

Most of the famous names in South African golf have at one time or other triumphed at the Wanderers. During the 1970s the field always included several of the top American golfers, further enhancing the prestige of the tournament. Two Americans, Tom Weiskopf and Hale Irwin, have each won the title. Another American winner was Corey Pavin in 1983, who went on from that triumph to greater feats in his home country. Irishman David Feherty was the victor in 1988. Dale Hayes won the PGA for three years in a row from

ABOVE AND OPPOSITE: *The par-four 9th hole, which is played as the closing hole during the annual PGA, travels uphill all the way through a narrow avenue of trees to the green guarded by two large bunkers.*

ABOVE: *The par-five 1st hole fairway and green.*
OPPOSITE: *The short 3rd hole features a water hazard next to the green.*

PGA CHAMPIONSHIP WINNERS

1972	Harold Henning (279)
1973	Tom Weiskopf (273)
1974	Dale Hayes (271)
1975	Dale Hayes (266)
1976	Dale Hayes (266)
1977	John Bland (275)
1978	Hale Irwin (275)
1979	Gary Player (203 over 54 holes)
1980	Hugh Baiocchi (268)
1981	(no tournament as the date was changed from November to January)
1982	Gary Player (272)
1983	Corey Pavin (270)
1984	Gavin Levenson (271)
1985	Chris Williams (272)
1986	Bobby Cole (265)
1987	Fulton Allem (268)
1988	David Feherty (267)
1989	Tony Johnstone (269)*
1990	Fulton Allem (266)
1991	Roger Wessels (271)**
1992	Ernie Els (271)
1993	Mark McNulty (265)

* Won play-off against Chris Williams
** Won play-off against Mark James and Hugh Royer

1974 to 1976, with a stroke average of 67 during that period, and Gary Player and Fulton Allem have had two victories apiece.

Player had to wait until 1979 for his first win at the Wanderers, in a tournament where the last round was washed out by rain. Two years later he defeated American Bill Rogers, the reigning British Open champion, McNulty, and Englishman Gordon Brand Junior, winning by three shots. Player clinched the title with an incredible 20-metre putt for a birdie at the 16th hole, after having to crawl through the surrounding spectators on all fours in order to reach the green.

During the PGA the holes are played in a different order to the usual club layout. The finishing hole is the club's 9th, and the par is cut to 70. The club par is 71 but for the PGA the short par-four 17th hole is reduced to a 220-metre par-three.

These changes were initiated by Pat McKenna, a past Wanderers' captain and chairman, and today a life member, who suggested to the PGA tournament director, Brian Henning, that the club's 18th was not a good finishing hole and that the 9th would be preferable, while also allowing more space for grandstands.

While hosting the PGA, the course has been continually upgraded to make it as challenging as possible, and new bunkers have been added to the layout over the years. The tree-lined fairways, which are narrow on most holes, place a premium on accurate driving. Long, straight shots off the tee can set up birdies most of the way round the course.

Two of the most difficult holes on the course are positioned right next to each other. The club's 10th hole is a long par-four of 459 metres. Play involves driving from an elevated tee into a slight depression and then facing an uphill shot to the green. It is the stroke-two hole.

The 423-metre 9th hole, which is played as the 18th hole in the PGA, travels uphill all the way, with a drive which has to be hit through a narrow avenue of trees. The base of the pin cannot be seen from the fairway, and judging the distance to the hole is a good test of depth perception.

The record score for the PGA is 15-under-par 265, which was attained by Bobby Cole in 1986 and matched by Mark McNulty in 1993. However, at least 10 of the winning totals have been at 270 or higher. Despite this, there have been some excellent individual scores. Dale Hayes held the course record of 62 for 15 years until Fulton Allem opened with 61 in the first round of the 1990 championship. Hayes' 62 in the third round of the 1975 PGA was additionally memorable for the fact that he displayed great sportsmanship by calling a penalty shot on himself at the 4th hole when his ball moved as he addressed it.

For the professional golfer, Wanderers is not the most testing course in South Africa. It is of moderate length for today's long-hitters, yet it demands exacting iron shots to small greens, all of which are very well bunkered. Water poses a serious hazard throughout the opening stretch: at the 1st hole, where a stream crosses in front of the green, at the 2nd hole where a dam follows the length of the fairway and at the short, 157-metre 3rd hole. Thus the course, which is set in pristine park-like conditions, demands precision play from start to finish.

OPPENHEIMER PARK GOLF CLUB

Designed by Robert Grimsdell

Oppenheimer Park Golf Club is a verdant oasis situated within the gold mining town of Welkom in the northern Free State, with lush fairways, bent-grass greens and a profusion of magnificent trees growing densely throughout the property. It has all the hallmarks of a championship layout and, played off the back tees, it is a lengthy test of golf, demanding accuracy particularly during the summer months when the rough flourishes and the fairways are narrowed down.

Named after one of South Africa's most prominent families, more than 40 years have passed since the course was opened by Harry Oppenheimer. Few South African golf courses are named after famous people, but it is appropriate in this instance as Oppenheimer Park Golf Club is owned and subsidized by the Anglo-American corporation, which was founded by Sir Ernest Oppenheimer.

Competitors in the first South African Amateur championship held at Oppenheimer Park in 1981 found it exceptionally severe, and a visit to the thick rough in the first round by Springbok Neil James ultimately cost him the 72-hole stroke play title. He took a nine on the par-four 15th hole, after

The green on the par-four 6th hole is closely guarded by a daunting water hazard.

OPPENHEIMER PARK GOLF CLUB

HOLES 18
DISTANCE 6 264 metres
PAR 72
RATING 71

HOLE	METRES	PAR	HOLE	METRES	PAR
1	418	4	10	389	4
2	347	4	11	479	5
3	177	3	12	175	3
4	500	5	13	359	4
5	335	4	14	479	5
6	361	4	15	364	4
7	146	3	16	335	4
8	346	4	17	141	3
9	511	5	18	402	4
OUT	**3 141**	**36**	**IN**	**3 123**	**36**

battling to get his ball back to the fairway, and in the end finished one shot behind the champion, Taiwanese golfer Ching-Chi Yuan. The winning score that year was three-over-par 291, a testimony to the difficult conditions.

Yuan was only the second golfer from outside southern Africa to win the national crown, Richard Langridge of Britain having captured the South African Amateur trophy in 1964, coincidentally at another Free State course, the Bloemfontein Golf Club. Bloemfontein and its neighbouring club, Schoeman Park, had previously hosted all the South African Amateurs and Opens held in the Orange Free State, until Oppenheimer Park was recognized in 1981.

The South African Amateur returned there in 1988, when Neville Clarke and Ernie Els competed in the second longest final in the history of the championship. They played to the 40th hole before Clarke won with a par-five to gain his second South African Amateur victory. The rough put paid to Els at this hole, and he was unable to reach the green in the required three shots.

Construction of the course, built on flat land next to a large dam, began in 1949, and the layout was officially opened in 1951.

One feature of the course is the abundance of trees lining the fairways, many of them exceptionally tall, and they punish any shot which strays off line. On the par-four 5th hole, the entrance to the

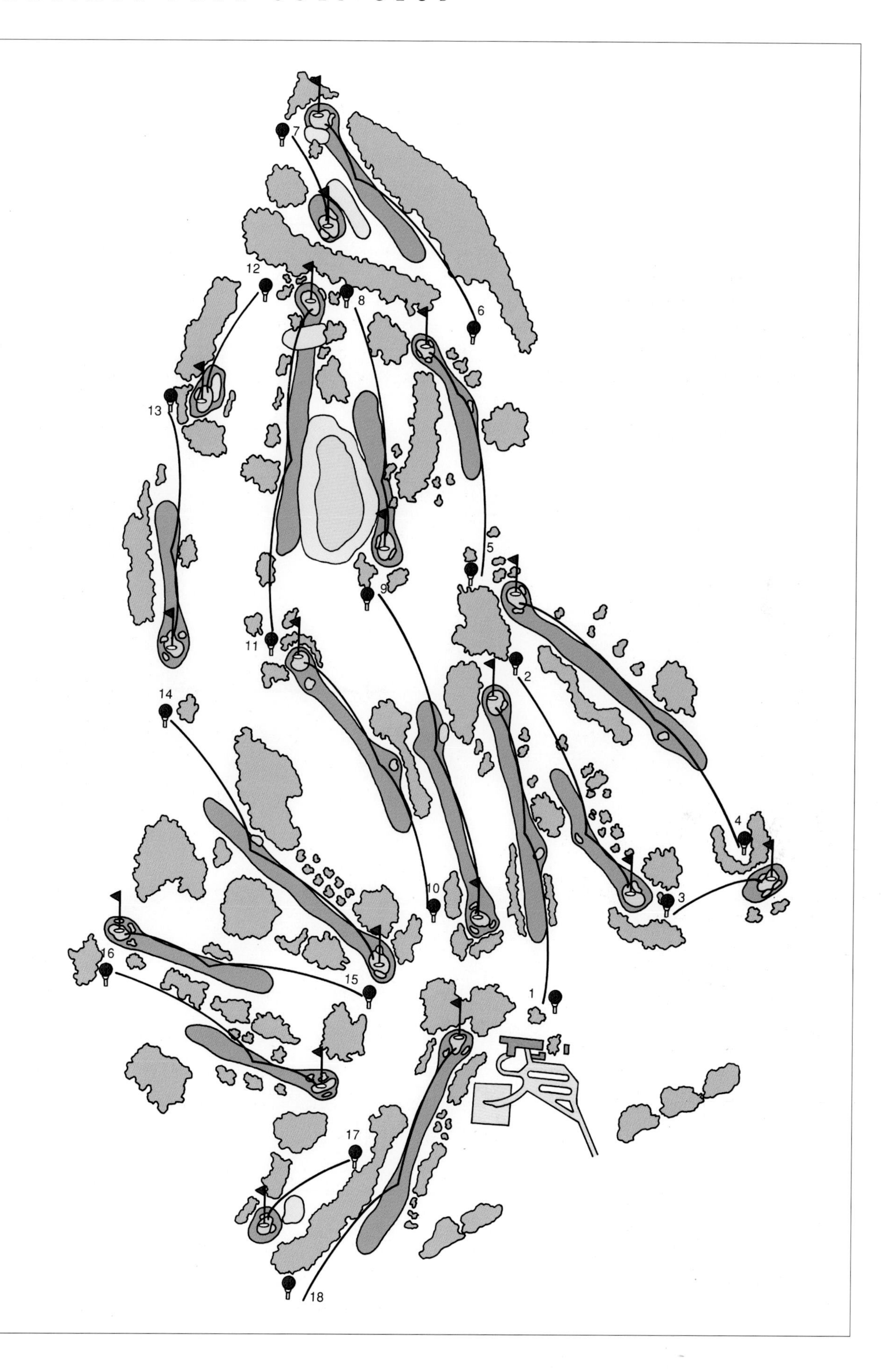

The water fronting the 17th green makes it a small, tricky target.

green is made exceedingly narrow by several enormous trees on the left-hand side of the fairway. The tee shot has to be kept to the right to avoid them.

Oppenheimer Park's two most difficult holes are at the start of each set of nine holes. The 1st hole is a straight but long par-four of 422 metres, and is the club's stroke two on the card. It takes two strong, accurate shots to reach the distant green. The 395-metre, par-four 10th hole is an even tougher prospect, a dogleg-left with trees to be avoided on the corner of the dogleg. The green is tucked away in a shady thicket, and is protected by bunkers in the front. It is justifiably the club's stroke-one hole.

The advantage of a difficult opening hole is that the course appears to become considerably easier thereafter, but it is a mistake to become complacent at Oppenheimer Park unless you are confident of playing well. The 2nd is a reasonably gentle par-four with a generously wide fairway, and the 3rd is a short par-three with a well-bunkered green. The par-five 4th is 504 metres in length, but it is fairly straightforward once the tee shot has been played clear of a large fairway bunker on the left.

The next four holes are among the prettiest and most challenging on the course. None of them are dauntingly long, yet they can pose problems. The 6th and 7th have water hazards guarding the greens, while the area around the 8th hole has been the scene of considerable refinement in recent years. A water hazard has been built to the right of the fairway, and the 8th is reasonably intimidating off the tee with the water and the trees making the fairway look uncomfortably narrow.

The 9th is the longest par-five on the course at 511 metres, running very slightly uphill to the one-storey, glass-fronted clubhouse which affords a superb outlook on the course. Following the 10th is yet another par-five, the 504-metre 11th, where a water hazard has been built in front of the green. Long-hitters can take up the challenge of clearing the water with two big shots. The 12th is without doubt the toughest par-three on the course, with a long-iron usually required to reach the big green which has a water hole cut into its left-hand side. Here the course runs alongside a sizable pan of water where huge flocks of flamingos – a feature of the area – can often be seen.

The 13th is a short par-four, but the green is well guarded in the front by bunkers. The par-five 14th, which moves away from the pan and is a slight dogleg-left, invites most golfers to attempt to reach the green in two shots. A well-struck drive with a draw along the left edge of the fairway can shorten the hole considerably, but there is a stand of tall trees and a fairway bunker on the corner of the dogleg, which have to be considered.

The 15th and 16th are similar-looking par-fours, and are followed by a hole which is the club's pride and joy, the short 17th. It is a delightful par-three, with water in front of the green making it an espe-

SOUTH AFRICAN AMATEUR WINNERS

1981	David Suddards
1988	Neville Clarke

SOUTH AFRICAN STROKE PLAY WINNERS

1981	Ching-Chi Yuan (291)
1988	Neville Clarke (283)

cially small target. The 18th is an outstanding finishing hole, a par-four of 407 metres, with a narrow fairway flanked by trees and a green which slopes severely from right to left.

Since first hosting the South African Amateur in 1981, big tournaments have become a regular feature at Oppenheimer Park, and the club is an annual host on the professional Winter Tour.

The club's crest is a large lizard, *Cordylus giganteus*, which is more locally known as the *Ou Volk* lizard. During construction they were found in abundance around the course. The 'Thursday Club' members are known as *Die Ou Volkers* (the old people) to this day.

The well-bunkered 4th green requires an accurate approach shot.

ABOVE LEFT AND RIGHT: *An eccentric feature of the course is the suggestion box situated in the water fronting the 17th green.*

DURBAN COUNTRY CLUB

Designed by George Waterman and Laurie Waters

Durban Country Club has reverential status to golfers the world over, and no South African golf course is as well known and celebrated outside this country. It has been admired by countless golfers who have had the opportunity of playing this challenging layout in its sub-tropical setting. The maintenance and condition of the Durban Country Club course has always been outstanding, and the indigenous Umgeni grass greens are generally considered to be among the finest and truest putting surfaces in the country.

Since it was built in 1922, however, this priceless asset on the Durban beachfront, close to the heart of the city, has been under constant threat from the city council, jealous of this prime land being occupied by a golf course.

Failing to recognize what an attraction they had in their midst, the council kept the club in fear of expropriation over the years with talk of schemes to develop the land for other purposes. Other clubs might have capitulated, but Durban Country Club members persevered in fighting the council so as not to concede their beautiful green lung to an expanding city.

An aerial view shows the gabled clubhouse overlooking the 18th green, with the 17th green in the foreground.

Durban Country Club originated through the necessity for a second golf course in Durban. Durban Golf Club (now Royal Durban Golf Club), situated on a low-lying swamp in the middle of Greyville racecourse, was subject to repeated flooding and was virtually unplayable during the 1919 South African championships. The championships were due to return to Durban in 1924, and the only way to ensure that the city would host them was to build another course. This urgent need resulted in a group of prominent Durban citizens deciding on the formation of a country club.

The land was found, but the town council would only lease it to the country club, thus setting in motion the problems that would be encountered in the years ahead. From the outset many councillors opposed the formation of Durban Country Club, and boycotted the official opening on 9 December 1922 as they had alternative plans for the area.

The first lease was for a period of 25 years, and in 1952 another 50-year lease was negotiated by the club. This lease, however, could be terminated by the city council at three years' notice, with no compensation. With this uncertainty surrounding the lease, in 1950 the club bought a splendid 157-acre stretch of land near Umhlanga Rocks for the possible development of another championship course, should the present one be expropriated.

The findings in the Holford Report of 1968 allayed many of the club's fears for the future. The report claimed it was essential to retain a permanent green lung amid the rapidly encroaching urban and industrial development. As recently as 1980, however, another councillor proposed a multi-million rand recreational scheme on the site of the course.

Only in recent years has the threat of expropriation receded, and Durban Country Club continues to maintain its status as South Africa's highest ranked course in the world ratings. In 1991 it had risen to 52nd place in *Golf Magazine*'s biennial rankings of top international golf courses.

Trapped between freeways and the Umgeni River, Durban Country Club has been diminished in size by a growing city, but is essentially still as attractive and tranquil as when it was first built. When playing over the undulating fairways, bordered by lush vegetation which includes several varieties of indigenous trees, it is hard to believe that the course is not in the middle of a remote tropical estate.

The course originated on a marsh bordering the beachfront and the Umgeni River, a natural site edged by giant dunes. This wasteland was transformed through the work of the two men who designed and constructed the course, George Waterman and Johannesburg Golf Club professional, Laurie Waters. The difficulties the two men faced in Durban were immense. All earthmoving had to be done by hand, but eventually the giant dunes were flattened and the dense bush and trees chopped down and removed.

DURBAN COUNTRY CLUB

HOLES 18
DISTANCE 6 074 metres
PAR 73
RATING 72

HOLE	METRES	PAR	HOLE	METRES	PAR
1	352	4	10	503	5
2	172	3	11	417	4
3	469	5	12	136	3
4	158	3	13	306	4
5	421	5	14	472	5
6	322	4	15	171	3
7	343	4	16	381	4
8	459	5	17	354	4
9	388	4	18	250	4
OUT	**3 084**	**37**	**IN**	**2 990**	**36**

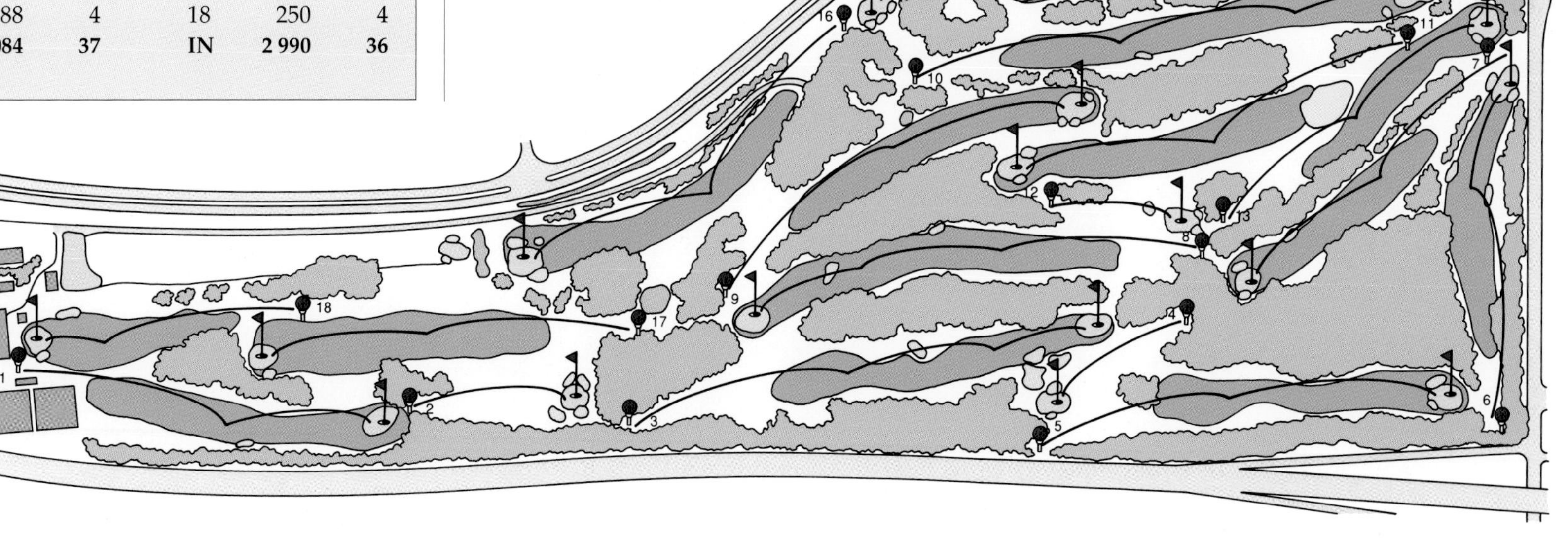

The green of the par-five 3rd hole, looking back through the valley to the tee.

Waterman is given most of the credit for the final masterpiece, and as a tribute to him the Waterman Cup was first competed for in 1924. It remains one of the leading golf trophies at the country club.

Although alterations have been made to the course over the years, the club has closely guarded the integrity of Waterman and Waters' basic design. English course architect Colonel S.V. Hotchkin suggested several changes during a visit in 1930, and in 1959 Robert Grimsdell was called in to make adjustments to the course, necessitated by the encroachment of principal roads and changing boundaries. Alterations were made to the 1st, 3rd, 9th, 10th and 11th holes.

Grimsdell was full of praise for Waterman's original design:

SOUTH AFRICAN OPEN WINNERS

1924	Bertie Elkin (316)
1928	Jock Brews (297)
1939	Bobby Locke (279)
1950	Bobby Locke (280)
1956	Gary Player (286)
1963	Retief Waltman (281)
1969	Gary Player (273)
1973	Bob Charles (282)
1976	Gary Player (280)
1980	Bobby Cole (279)
1988	Wayne Westner (275)
1991	Wayne Westner (272)*

* Equalled the record South African Open winning total and the lowest at the coast.

SOUTH AFRICAN AMATEUR WINNERS

1924	Leslie Forster
1928	Bernard Wynne
1933	Clarence Olander
1939	Otway Hayes
1950	Eric Dalton
1956	Reg Taylor
1963	Dave Symons
1971	Coen Dreyer
1978	Teddy Webber

SOUTH AFRICAN STROKE PLAY WINNERS

1971	Kevin Suddards (291)
1978	David Suddards (290)

'The course was laid out at a time when golf course architecture was in its infancy and was only beginning to achieve recognition as a profession,' remarked Grimsdell. 'Waterman was untrained in the art of golf course architecture, yet he revealed an instinctive appreciation of nature's work, and he succeeded in producing an outstanding result.' (From *The First 60 Years 1922 to 1982* by Joyce Wrinch-Schulz.)

The South African Golf Union certainly considered Durban Country Club an essential part of their championship roster. The club has hosted more South African Opens than any other club – 12 in all – between 1924 and 1991. It was also the venue for the first interprovincial tournament, which was held in 1960.

The 1928 South African Open saw one of the most exciting finishes in the history of the championship. Jock Brews needed to play the last four holes level par to tie with his brother Sid, but

The 8th fairway travels through an undulating valley to an elevated green.

carded a five at the 17th hole. A birdie three was required at the 18th hole, a short par-four that presents an unusual finish to a strenuous layout. At 252 metres in length it encourages the bold player to go for the green with the tee shot. Jock Brews did just that, hitting a magnificent drive just three metres from the hole, then holing the putt for an eagle to beat his brother by one shot.

Sid Brews was Durban Country Club's first professional, from 1924 to 1934, before he left for Houghton. Since then, the club has had only three other professionals: Bob Broadley, Jimmy Ockenden and the present incumbent, Hugh Inggs.

The five opening holes at Durban Country Club are considered to be among the toughest on the course, and they can be unforgiving. The 1st is a relatively short but tight par-four, and the par-three 2nd hole is played from a high tee to a green built on the ridge of a dune.

The par-five 3rd is played from another elevated tee into a glorious valley with mounds and undulations all the way to the green. There are several of these lofty tees on the course, each giving a sweeping view of the holes below.

Situated on the beachfront, Durban Country Club is trapped between freeways and the encroaching city.

The short 4th hole, measuring 158 metres, turns in the opposite direction towards a sunken green. In the club's early years the green was completely hidden from the tee by a hill, and strangely there was a remarkably high proportion of holes-in-one. That was until it was discovered that caddies were placing the ball in the cup, knowing full well that they would be handsomely rewarded! Thereafter, caddies were required to stand within sight of the tee, and eventually the top of the hill, which obscured the green, was removed to give a direct view of the pin.

The long par-four 5th hole is one of the most fearsome holes on the course. The tee is perched tight against the boundary fence, with a long carry to a narrow fairway.

The 6th hole offers a good chance of a birdie, whereas the 7th, while not very long, requires an accurate tee shot through an avenue of trees to a green that is tucked away in a clearing.

The 8th is another par-five hole, with a distance of 459 metres, running parallel but in the opposite direction to the 3rd. The green is situated at the top of a sand hill next to the high tee of the 9th, a hole which is often underestimated, with its fairway curving to the right

The back nine begins with the longest par-five on the course, an intimidating 503-metre stretch with its raised target a long, narrow green. The 11th hole is another strong par-four, equal in strength to the 5th, although more open.

One of the earlier overseas visitors to Durban Country Club was the Prince of Wales in 1925, who made what is now the 12th hole (at that time it was the 10th hole) famous by taking 17 shots on it. The hole, affectionately known as the Prince of Wales, is only 136 metres in length, but the narrow green is perched on top of a mound with a steep drop on either side. The Prince repeatedly hit his ball from one side of the green to the other before holing out. Obviously no-one present had the presumption to tell him to pick up the ball. The Prince presented the club with another of its major trophies, the Prince of Wales Cup.

The 13th hole is played from the top of another hill, under the shade of an ancient fig tree, and long-hitters can almost drive the green downwind. The 14th hole is a straightforward par-five if one can stick to the fairway, and the short 15th has a tightly bunkered green.

A testing dogleg-right par-four, the 16th is a redesigned hole completed in 1980, and is an improvement on the old 16th which was played to a plateau green.

The 17th is an innovative hole in that the fairway is a switchback of deep depressions. From the bottom of one of these there is no sight of the green, so the correct tee shot should be played to a flat area to the right of the fairway.

Durban Country Club is much more than just a golf club. The magnificent gabled clubhouse has been a hub of Durban social activity for many years. Peter van Diggelen, secretary from 1955 to 1976, is long remembered with affection by both members and staff. He had a great influence on the club, not only in an organizational capacity, but in promoting social activities. The club offers other sporting facilities such as tennis, bowls and squash, and the clubhouse provides ceaseless entertainment for members. The popularity of the club is more than obvious from the fact that it has a current membership of 11 000 and a lengthy waiting list stretching many years ahead.

The 12th hole, with its narrow green perched on top of a steep mound.

The par-three 15th hole plays to a narrow, tightly bunkered green.

MARITZBURG COUNTRY CLUB

Designed by Robert Grimsdell

Maritzburg Country Club is one of the most picturesque of South Africa's golf courses, very English in its setting and entirely appropriate in design for this area of Natal. It is a parkland course with breathtaking views, set on the slopes of the beautiful, hilly countryside on the outskirts of the city of Pietermaritzburg.

Pietermaritzburg has the second oldest golf club in South Africa, the Maritzburg Golf Club, which was founded in 1886. Maritzburg Country Club was established 45 years later on the sloping grasslands adjoining Queen Elizabeth Park.

This new course, opened in 1933, had grass greens, which up to then had not been introduced to the Maritzburg Golf Club layout at Scottsville. Ironically, the country club course is now a good deal older than the present Maritzburg Golf Club course. After 60 years of playing golf in Scottsville, the university appropriated the land for extensions and in 1970 the Maritzburg Golf Club moved to its fourth location, in the Hay Paddock area. This was also designed by Robert Grimsdell.

Grimsdell was responsible for the redesigning of the Maritzburg Country Club course in 1935 and, as usual, he made his mark with the creation of a wonderful variety of holes which cleverly utilize the hilly landscape. Significant alterations were

The clubhouse and the 10th (foreground) and 18th (right) greens, set against the rolling countryside on the outskirts of Pietermaritzburg.

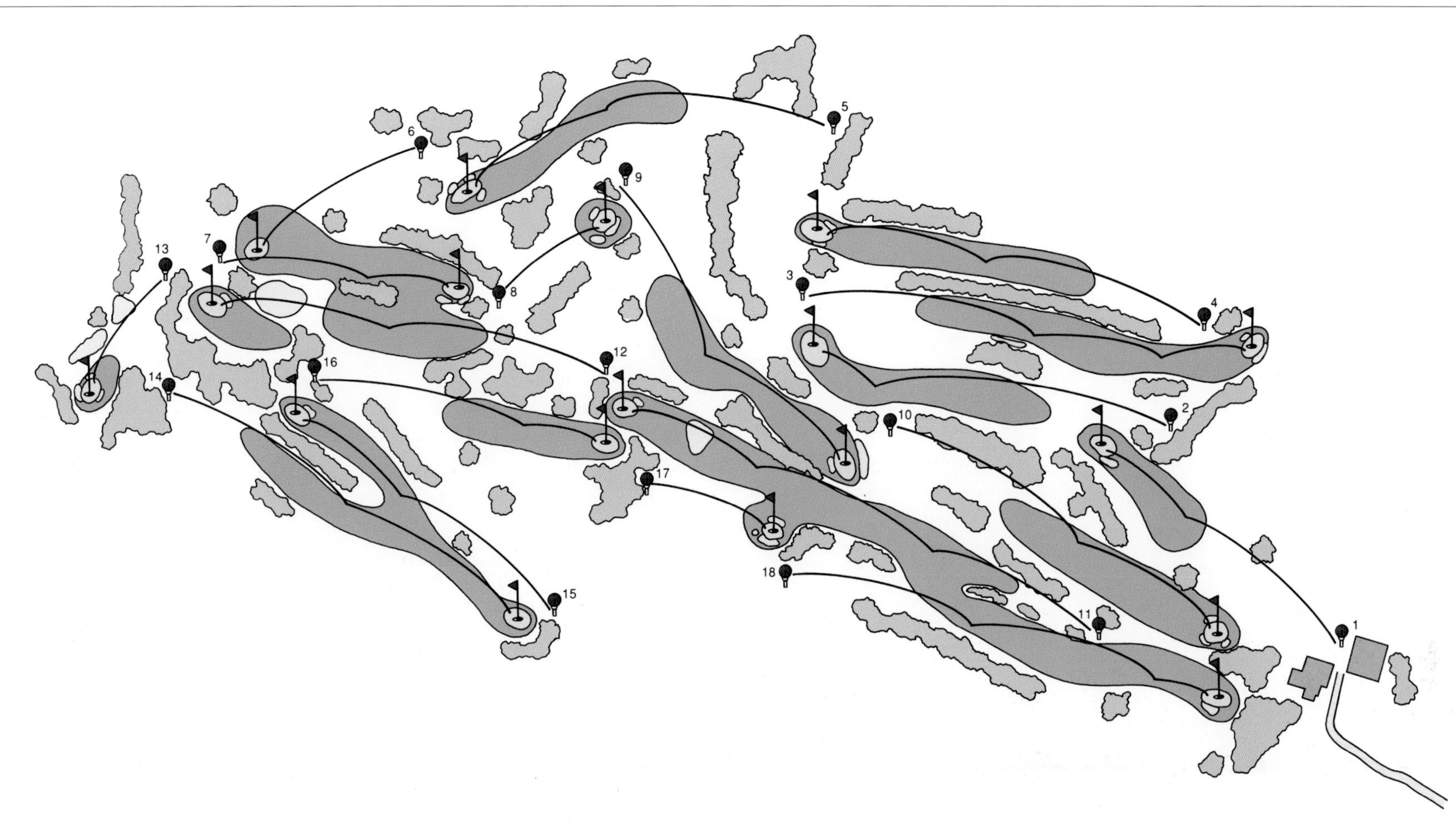

MARITZBURG COUNTRY CLUB

HOLES 18
DISTANCE 6 115 metres
PAR 71
RATING 71

HOLE	METRES	PAR	HOLE	METRES	PAR
1	313	4	10	382	4
2	374	4	11	530	5
3	490	5	12	420	4
4	412	4	13	136	3
5	396	4	14	424	4
6	208	3	15	332	4
7	246	4	16	306	4
8	158	3	17	148	3
9	378	4	18	462	5
OUT	**2 975**	**35**	**IN**	**3 140**	**36**

also made in 1965, using thousands of tons of surplus soil from the national highway which winds its way up Town Hill above the course.

The 18 holes at Maritzburg Country Club are primarily a combination of long and short par-fours, with nothing in between. It has no fewer than seven extremely tough par-fours, the shortest of these being 375 metres and the longest 424 metres. As most of them play uphill, they present a tough challenge. These are offset by four short par-fours, of between 246 and 332 metres in length.

The clubhouse, an attractive blend of old and modern architecture, stands on a ridge overlooking the course, and the 1st hole drops spectacularly from a high tee into a valley. At 313 metres, there is the inevitable temptation to try and drive as close to the green as possible. This hole is a relatively easy introduction to the course, but there is no further respite until the 7th hole.

The 2nd to the 6th is a formidable stretch, the easiest hole probably being the 490-metre, par-five 3rd hole, curving through the valley to a target which does not reveal itself until cresting a rise near the green. The tee shot is played from the top of a hill, affording another good view of the surroundings, but the second shot is a blind one over the rise.

The 4th and 5th are superb par-fours, both requiring long accurate drives followed by a medium or long-iron to the green. The 4th, at 412 metres, does not attempt to conceal itself, being a straight hole lined by tall trees, but beware of the out-of-bounds area on the right. The 5th is fractionally shorter but plays as long, being a dogleg-left to an elevated green set at the top of a slope.

Having climbed the hill to the 5th green and then coped with its sharply contoured surface, the 6th hole comes as a further blow. This is a 208-metre par-three with a green set on the edge of a steep grassy bank. The tee shot has to be kept to the left to avoid rolling down this bank.

There is a touch of old-fashioned English eccentricity about the 7th. The tee is set immediately behind the 6th green and a low shot could easily carom off the flagstick. Measuring 246 metres, a long, straight shot can find the green. The fairway is a narrow one, however, with the ground falling away down a steep slope on the left, and with massive trees on the right, so it is just as easy to bogey the hole as it is to birdie it.

The short 8th is played from an elevated tee, and is followed by another pair of long par-fours climbing uphill to the clubhouse. Ten holes are completed before arriving at the halfway house, an eccentric feature of this course which is also to be found at East London Golf Club.

The 9th hole doglegs left and has an intimidating, large green which features a water hazard ready to catch any hooked approach. The fairway on the 10th slopes from right to left, and the rolling contours leave a blind second shot to the green.

The 530-metre 11th hole is a memorable par-five. The tee shot is played downhill and, if this shot is long enough, with the second shot you can attempt to carry a strategically placed water hazard. Most golfers lay-up, leaving a short-iron approach to the small green. The 12th also has a big dam, but this is placed just short of the green. At 420 metres it is a long carry to the flag from the fairway. There is nothing too intimidating about the short 13th, but the same cannot be said of the tough 14th, the club's stroke one at 424 metres. The tee shot has to navig-

ABOVE: *The par-four 5th, with its undulating, dogleg-left fairway ascending to the elevated green.*

OPPOSITE: *Played from an elevated tee through a depression, the short 8th hole requires an accurate approach shot to avoid the bunkers surrounding the raised green.*

The spectacular scenery is shown to good advantage from the 3rd and 4th fairways.

The 12th hole's fairway and green, showing the lush, sub-tropical vegetation typical of this parkland course.

SUNSHINE CIRCUIT TOURNAMENT WINNER

1973	John Fourie (213)

SOUTH AFRICAN AMATEUR WINNER

1989	Craig Rivett

SOUTH AFRICAN STROKE PLAY WINNER

1989	Ernie Els (279)

ate clumps of trees and the fairway ambles uphill to an elevated green.

Having passed the 14th, the finish is decidedly less arduous. But while the holes are shorter from here on, they are no less tight and care must still be taken. The uneven nature of the fairways tends to deflect balls in the direction of the rough and the trees. The course ends with a 462-metre par-five which climbs up a hill and drops down the other side to the green. Thick rough and a lateral water hazard make the right-hand side an unpleasant place to visit.

Oddly enough, for a layout of such stature, the Maritzburg Country Club was passed over as a South African championship venue until 1989, when the South African Amateur was held there. It proved itself a worthy test, with Ernie Els' winning 72-hole stroke play score being five-under-par for the par-71 layout.

The 36-hole final of the match play that year for the Amateur trophy produced a stirring contest between Els and his main Transvaal rival, Craig Rivett. Els was three down with five holes to play but levelled the match on the 36th hole. He made his third consecutive birdie on the 37th, but that was only good for a half and he lost at the 38th when he missed a short putt. Els had become the youngest winner of the South African Amateur at East London in 1986, at the age of sixteen years and five months, but he was never to win the crown again, despite playing in four successive finals. Maritzburg Country Club was to be his last appearance in the event.

OPPOSITE: *Maritzburg Country Club course does justice to the picturesque countryside surrounding it. The undulating terrain provides a variety of sloping holes, and makes for a challenging and enjoyable round of golf.*

MOUNT EDGECOMBE COUNTRY CLUB

Designed by William Campbell

Mount Edgecombe Country Club has been in existence for almost 60 years, but the whole shape of the property has changed in the last two years, with luxury homes being built alongside the fairways in the increasingly popular tradition of American golfing estates.

Mount Edgecombe is in fact the third name given to this country club on the Natal north coast. It was first known as Natal Estates Golf Club, the development of which came about because the employees of the surrounding sugar estates found it an arduous undertaking to drive from Mount Edgecombe to Durban for a round of golf.

The original nine-hole course, designed by William Campbell, was expanded to an 18-hole layout in 1935. One of the primary movers behind the development of the full course was H.V. Franklin, honorary greenkeeper from the club's inception until 1960. The club later changed to Huletts Country Club, which many South Africans became familiar with over the years. It takes its latest name, Mount Edgecombe, from the area itself.

Although not far from the sea, and therefore susceptible to strong winds, the course has a parkland aspect, and is host to a wonderful variety of large trees and sub-tropical vegetation. The redesigned Mount Edgecombe layout is an attractive

Following the American tradition of golfing estates, Mount Edgecombe combines an outstanding country club with a beautiful residential area.

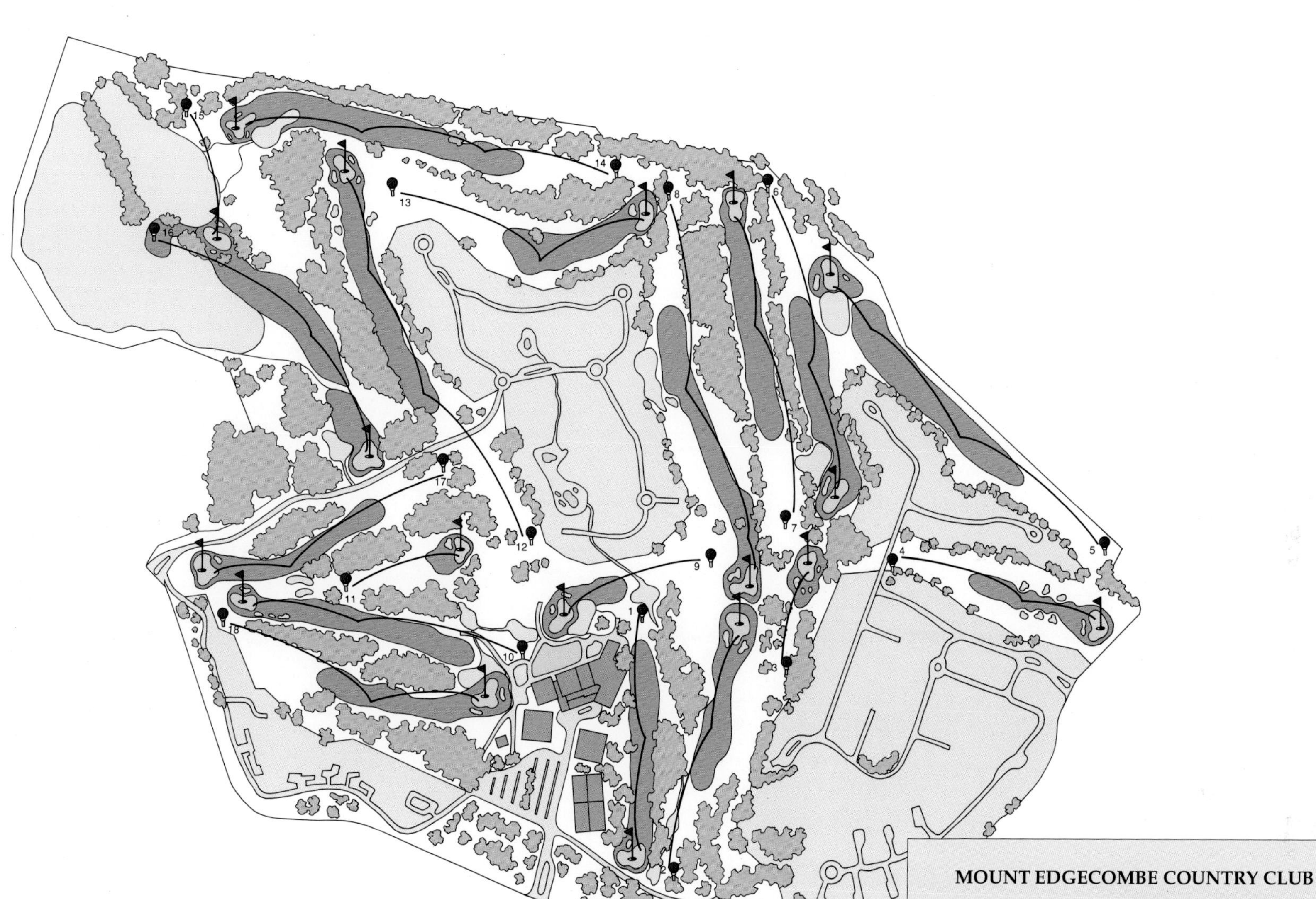

addition to the growing number of estate courses in South Africa. It incorporates several new holes, and the others have had their greens reshaped.

Huletts was always regarded as a good championship test, and hosted the Rothmans men's interprovincial in 1975 and 1987, as well as the South African Women's Amateur in 1980. The course was famous for its small, tricky greens which were difficult to read. In comparison, the new greens are vast and contoured, and can accommodate a variety of pin positions. The greens have been planted with the same type of grass that has made Durban Country Club's greens among the finest in South Africa, and considerable skill is still required on the greens to return a good score.

Highly respected South African professional golfer, Hugh Baiocchi, who recently ventured into golf course architecture, designed the changes to the layout in partnership with Tony Falkson and Alan Barnard, who are from Natal. Between them they have upgraded the course in accordance with the best of modern standards. Mount Edgecombe,

MOUNT EDGECOMBE COUNTRY CLUB

HOLES 72
DISTANCE 6 180 metres
PAR 72
RATING 72

HOLE	METRES	PAR	HOLE	METRES	PAR
1	303	4	10	364	4
2	336	4	11	195	3
3	154	3	12	513	5
4	267	4	13	340	4
5	479	5	14	476	5
6	383	4	15	168	3
7	405	4	16	408	4
8	505	5	17	333	4
9	193	3	18	358	4
OUT	**3 025**	**36**	**IN**	**3 155**	**36**

Spectacular water hazards, such as this pond separating the 1st green and the 2nd tee, are a feature of this verdant course.

with many of its well-bunkered holes flanked by tall bluegum and pine trees, is a rewarding course for the accurate golfer, rather than the long-hitter.

The 1st hole immediately confirms this. Measuring 303 metres, it is a shortish par-four, but is an intimidating tee shot with which to begin a round. The fairway narrows in the driving area, with an out-of-bounds on the right and a thick plantation of pine trees on the left. The 2nd hole is of similar length, returning parallel to the 1st, but with plenty of room on the right.

The 3rd is an attractive 154-metre par-three which is highly rated and respected by the club members. The tee shot is played through an avenue of trees to a narrow green which is surrounded by bunkers, presenting a tiny target.

The 4th, 5th and 6th are entirely new holes, very different from each other. The 4th hole is a short par-four, the 5th hole is a downhill par-five, and the 6th hole is a longer, rather testing par-four. They replace the old 6th, 7th and 8th holes. The 6th and 7th used to be back-to-back par-fives, while the 8th hole was a short par-four. This triangular area has now been converted to a residential area. The fairway on the 4th appears to be as narrow as the green on the 3rd hole, with bunkers flanking both sides most of the way to the green. At 267 metres it

MOUNT EDGECOMBE TROPHY WINNER

1993 Retief Goosen (279)

is short enough to tempt the longer-hitters to try for the green.

The par-five 5th is a fearsome and challenging hole, with the prevailing wind usually blowing across the fairway. The tee shot has to be played to suit the wind. It is not a particularly long hole, but it can yield a double-bogey seven just as easily as a birdie four. The boundary wall of the property forms an out-of-bounds on the right, and the residential area does the same on the left. The fairway falls sharply downhill towards a big green protected by a water hazard on the front left. It is a hole to be treated with respect in a medal round, but is worth a bold effort in match play.

The 6th hole also has a big pond guarding the green although, as with the 5th, there is the option of avoiding it down one side. The 405-metre, par-four 7th hole requires the second shot to be played to an elevated green, and judging the approach to the pin can be problematic.

In order to keep the par at 72, the old 5th hole, now the 8th, has been lengthened to a 505-metre par-five, still retaining its dogleg off the tee. It requires a draw to find the middle of the fairway.

The new green on the par-three 9th has been repositioned, making it a much longer and tougher hole than the old 9th. Here another water hazard lies in wait for any shot that is played short.

The back nine has experienced fewer changes, and follows the old Huletts layout faithfully. The 10th hole is an undemanding par-four, the 11th is another exacting par-three, and the 12th hole is a 513-metre, dogleg par-five where the fairway sweeps past towering bluegum trees.

The 340-metre 13th is the start of an interesting stretch of holes. The fairway on this par-four turns sharply left near the driving area. It requires a good tee shot to have sight of the green which is situated at the top of a rise. This two-level green was one of the most treacherous of the old greens.

The next three holes were the pride and joy of Huletts because at that time they were the only holes with water hazards. They were referred to as the club's 'Amen Corner', as they often dictated the

A view of the 6th and 7th holes, which run adjacent to each other.

Immaculately maintained greens are a feature of this Natal course.

The Natal-Victorian style clubhouse has a magnificent outlook over the course.

The new 9th green, featuring bunkers and a water hazard.

outcome of a round. Their challenge has not diminished and they are still described as such.

The 14th is a downhill par-five, which has been shortened to encourage the bold player to carry the pond fronting the green with his second shot. The fairway is generously wide, but the drive must hug the right-hand side, as anything to the left encounters a dense stand of bluegum trees blocking the view of the green.

The 15th is possibly the club's signature hole, a 168-metre par-three with nothing but water from tee to green. It is played from a high tee, giving a dramatic outlook over the hole. The excitement continues with the 16th – an equally daunting hole. For this long, 408-metre par-four, the drive has to be played over another big dam to the fairway. The tee itself has been built out on to the edge of the water, which makes the drive doubly intimidating. The hole doglegs right, and the more water that is carried with the tee shot, the shorter the next shot will be to the green.

Tall pines are again a feature on the 17th hole, standing sentinel on the right-hand side of the fairway. At 333 metres, this is not an unduly taxing par-four; however it possesses a notoriously difficult green that slopes downhill from back to front.

The 18th is a fine finishing hole, curving left through the trees, and strengthened by a treacherously undulating green and a new water hazard to the left of it.

Behind the 18th green stands the new clubhouse, a Natal-Victorian style building with a magnificent outlook over the course from its upper ground-floor areas. It is an improvement on the previous clubhouse, which was destroyed by fire in 1988 and did not offer a view of the impressive 18th hole from any of its entertainment areas.

While some may feel that part of the countrified charm and beauty of the old Huletts has disappeared with the new property development, the present layout provides South Africa with an excellent championship course of international standard. In fact, Mount Edgecombe recently hosted its first professional tournament, the inaugural Mount Edgecombe Trophy, as part of the 1993 Sunshine Tour.

OPPOSITE: *The tree-lined 10th fairway leading to the well-bunkered green, with the 17th green on the right.*

ROYAL DURBAN GOLF CLUB

Designed by Robert Grimsdell

Situated in the centre of the famous Greyville racecourse in the heart of Durban, 1992 saw Royal Durban Golf Club celebrate the centenary of the first holes to be built at this special sporting site. Although Royal Durban Golf Club has played second fiddle in hosting the South African championships throughout the century to neighbouring Durban Country Club, it is nevertheless a magnificent championship course. Looking at the scorecard the course does not appear overly long, but the lush kikuyu fairways offer very little run.

On first impression the course may appear featureless within the boundaries of the racecourse, with few trees and little definition, but the holes have been masterfully laid out and are exposed to the wind, providing an interesting challenge.

Two major and ever-present hazards are the out-of-bounds and the wide stormwater drainage canal that runs through the middle of the course. Between them they account for many a penalty shot. The rough can also be grown to a fearsome thickness and proved a nightmare for competitors during the 1985 South African Open, which was won by Gavin Levenson.

Close to the heart of Durban, Royal Durban Golf Club is situated within the famous Greyville racecourse.

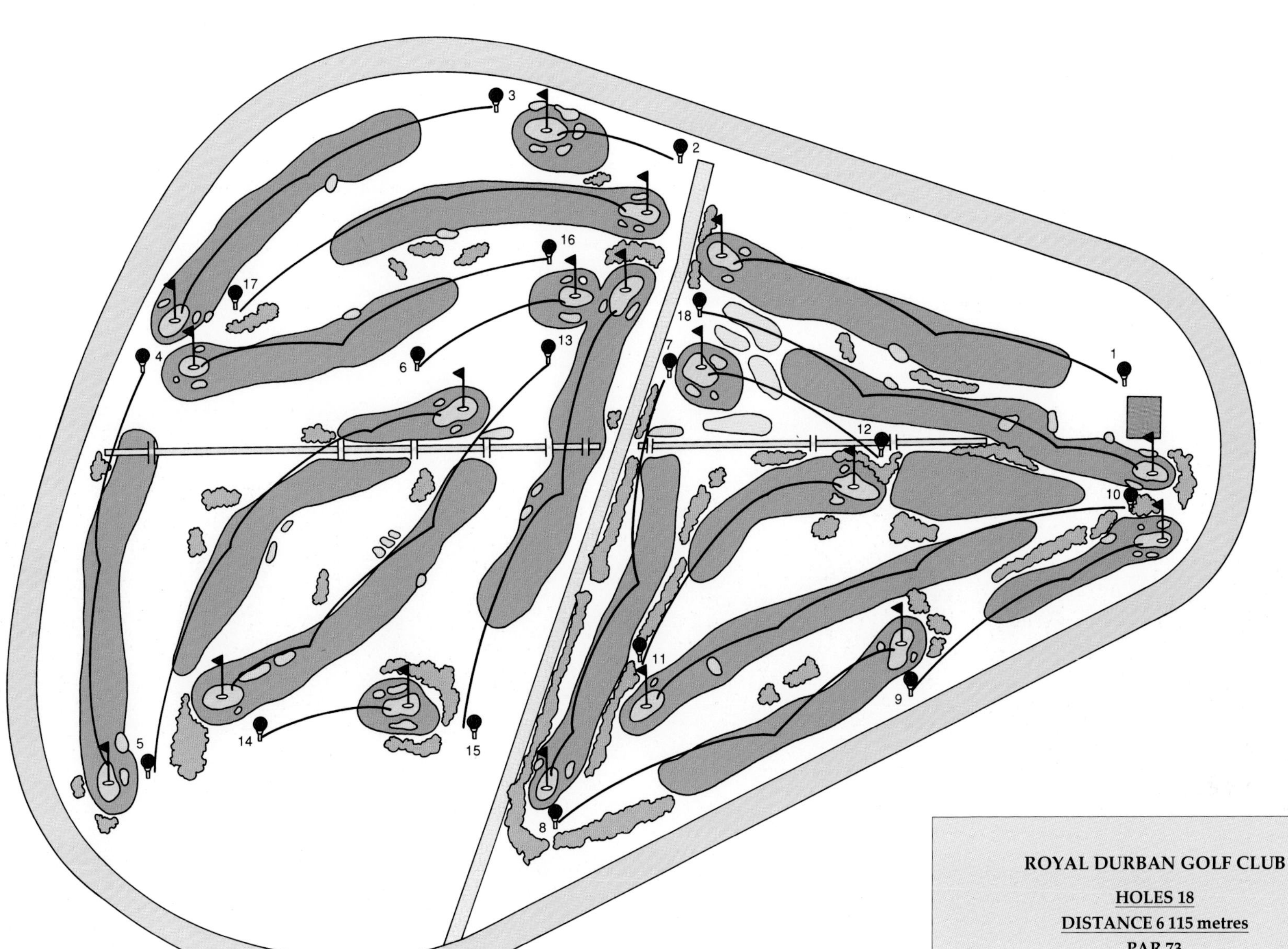

ROYAL DURBAN GOLF CLUB

HOLES 18
DISTANCE 6 115 metres
PAR 73
RATING 72

HOLE	METRES	PAR	HOLE	METRES	PAR
1	380	4	10	483	5
2	140	3	11	278	4
3	392	4	12	174	3
4	377	4	13	440	5
5	465	5	14	161	3
6	173	3	15	409	4
7	428	5	16	349	4
8	371	4	17	388	4
9	265	4	18	442	5
OUT	**2 991**	**36**	**IN**	**3 124**	**37**

Durban Golf Club started out as a scruffy nine-hole course in 1892, and for many years it was a rough layout and was prone to flooding during heavy rain, having been built on what was originally a marsh, hence the construction of the much-needed stormwater drain.

The club hosted two South African championships, in 1911 and 1919, but after the opening of the Durban Country Club it was not used again as a South African Open venue until 1970.

The club's professional at the time, George Fotheringham, won the first South African Open championship to be played in Durban in 1911. It was the third of his five Open triumphs between 1908 and 1914, after which he emigrated to the United States. Fotheringham assisted in the design of the course during its formative years.

A momentous occasion in the history of the club occurred in April 1932, when King George V granted the club permission to use the prefix

'Royal'. It was the fourth and final club in South Africa to attain this distinction, following Royal Cape (1910), Royal Port Alfred (1924) and Royal Johannesburg (1931).

The beautiful clubhouse at Royal Durban Golf Club was rebuilt in the 1930s, and in 1935 the decision was taken to invite the leading golf course architect of that era, Robert Grimsdell, to improve and redesign the existing layout of the course. The result of his work is the course that is in existence today, although he returned to Royal Durban in the early 1960s to further modernize the holes.

The club is entered through a historical gateway which stands as a memorial to those members who lost their lives during the First and Second World Wars. The clubhouse is a distinguished piece of

ABOVE: *On race days, golfers have an enviable view of the action from the 2nd green.*

OPPOSITE: *The par-four 15th is justifiably the club's stroke-one hole.*

The beautiful clubhouse was rebuilt in the 1930s.

SOUTH AFRICAN OPEN WINNERS

1911	George Fotheringham (301)
1919	W.H. Horne (320)
1970	Tommy Horton (285)
1985	Gavin Levenson (280)

SOUTH AFRICAN AMATEUR WINNERS

1911	Jimmy Prentice
1919	H. Gordon Stewart
1983	Ching-Chi Yuan
1992	Bradley Davison

SOUTH AFRICAN STROKE PLAY WINNERS

1983	Peter van der Riet (288)*
1992	John Nelson (284)

*Won play-off against Chin-Chan Yu and Duncan Lindsay-Smith

architecture, with a long veranda which overlooks the course.

The front nine take in the perimeter of the course, bordering the racetrack in an anti-clockwise direction. It does not pay to slice the ball at Royal Durban as the out-of-bounds area looms on the right-hand side of the course for most of the front nine. Where the par-five 5th hole provides a respite from the out-of-bounds, the stormwater drain emerges as a hazard.

Although the 1st hole is a straightforward par-four, it demands caution as there is an out-of-bounds fence which runs along the right edge of the fairway from tee to green. In addition, a new water hole has been built to the left of the green. From there the first of four crossings of Epsom Road, which runs through the middle of the course and under the racetrack, is encountered.

The 1st hole is followed by a delightful stretch: the 2nd is a well-bunkered short hole measuring 140 metres, and the 3rd and 4th holes call for accurately placed tee shots. Playing this section of the course during a race meeting at Greyville is always exciting, as it affords an impressive view of the horses as they gallop past these holes towards the finishing straight.

The 5th hole, measuring 465 metres, is a relatively short par-five and a good drive leaves the green within reach in two shots. However, the canal which diagonally crosses the fairway near the green has to be carried.

The par-three holes at Royal Durban offer a good variety of tee shots and the 6th is possibly the toughest at 173 metres from the back tee, with its slightly elevated, tightly bunkered green.

The 428-metre 7th is one of those holes often found at coastal courses which is neither a par-four nor a par-five. For club purposes it is a par-five but it is occasionally shortened to a par-four during championships. It is played parallel to Epsom Road and any shot which does not find the closely mown grass is caught by trees or hedgerows.

The next two holes hug the rails of the racetrack and two straight tee shots are required. The 8th hole is another solid par-four with a large sloping green, while the par-four, 265-metre 9th, is a possible birdie hole.

On the back nine it is a relief to play in the middle of the course and the three par-fives help improve scores. The 10th is the longest of these holes and has a tricky plateau green. The 11th hole is a short dogleg-right par-four, again with a difficult green which is best approached from the front.

The par-three 12th hole, recently made more difficult by the building of water hazards to catch any wayward shot, is played in the opposite direction to the 6th and is roughly the same length. If the wind is blowing hard, one of them is usually played with a short-iron, the other possibly with a wooden club. The par-five 13th hole presents a good chance of a birdie, and one which is definitely needed at that stage with a tough finish looming. The short 14th hole possesses a narrow green, which is once again raised, making recovery extremely difficult if the tee shot is not on target.

The par-four 15th is regarded as one of the toughest holes on the course. Apart from being long, it features a combination of the two main hazards – the road to the right and the drainage canal which has to be crossed. With the addition of fairway bunkers and mounds, and a contoured green, one has to be pleased with a four. The 16th

An aerial view of the 6th and 15th greens in the foreground, with the water hazards surrounding the 12th green on the far side of Epsom Road.

and 17th holes run parallel to each other, the former playing reasonably short, and the latter long and slightly uphill.

Like the 18th hole at Royal Johannesburg Golf Club, the closing hole at Royal Durban is a par-five and one which Gary Player has described as among the best in the country. The fairway curves back to the clubhouse and long-hitters can reach the large green in two shots.

A dramatic tournament finish occurred at this closing hole during the 1972 Natal Open, when Bobby Cole eagled the hole to beat Dale Hayes by one shot. Cole's winning total of 277 marked the first occasion that 280 had been broken over 72 holes. Just over nine years later, Mark McNulty bettered that total by one shot, scoring 276 with four consecutive rounds of 69 during a Sunshine Circuit tournament.

In 1975 the club hosted the last Commonwealth tournament to be played in South Africa, between the Springboks, Canada, New Zealand, Great Britain and Ireland. This tournament had the further distinction of being the first golf event to be televised in South Africa.

Royal Durban Golf Club was again the venue of the South African Amateur tournament in 1992, its centenary year, after an interval of nine years.

SELBORNE COUNTRY CLUB

Designed by Denis Barker

Selborne Country Club, set in the verdant, rolling countryside of the Natal south coast near Scottburgh, is a dream come true for its owner and course designer, Denis Barker. Anticipating the growing popularity of golf in South Africa in the 1980s, he transformed his dairy farm into one of the most spectacular golfing estates in the country. Beautiful indigenous trees line the fairways of this new addition to South Africa's leading courses, water hazards are a feature on virtually every hole, and the layout itself is immaculately maintained.

It is the emphasis on quality that makes Selborne Country Club stand out. The entrance to the estate creates an immediate impression of opulence, with trim avenues leading to a modern clubhouse and the double-storeyed lodge, which is an exclusive country guest house. Featuring hand-hewn stone, the lodge resembles an English manor house. On entering, a glimpse of the 17th green with its modern contouring and superb putting surface, promises an exciting game of golf.

Denis Barker designed and built the 18-hole course on his own land, turned his family home into a luxury country lodge and encouraged

The 18th green, lined with palm trees, is overlooked by the double-storey lodge.

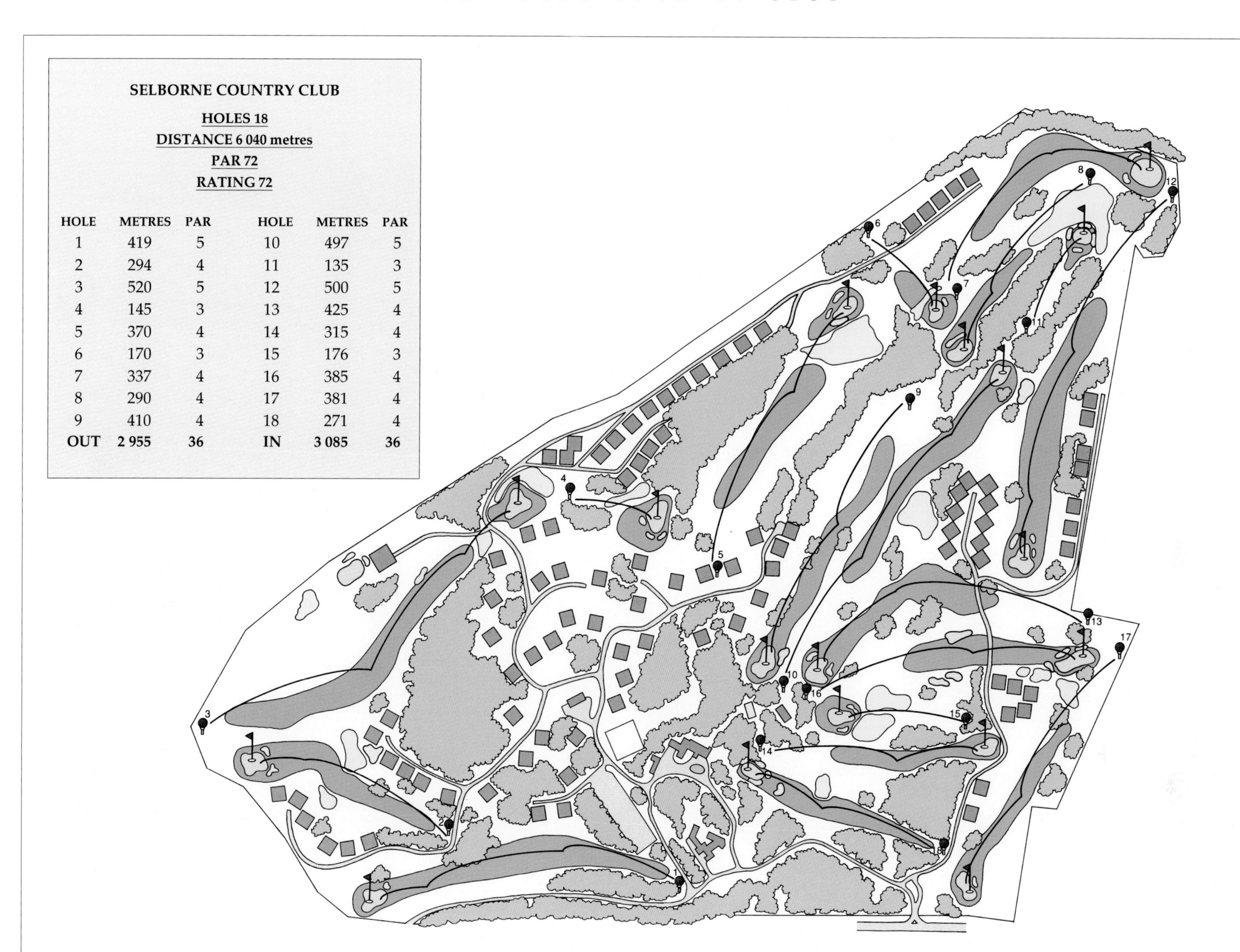

SELBORNE COUNTRY CLUB

HOLES 18
DISTANCE 6 040 metres
PAR 72
RATING 72

HOLE	METRES	PAR	HOLE	METRES	PAR
1	419	5	10	497	5
2	294	4	11	135	3
3	520	5	12	500	5
4	145	3	13	425	4
5	370	4	14	315	4
6	170	3	15	176	3
7	337	4	16	385	4
8	290	4	17	381	4
9	410	4	18	271	4
OUT	**2 955**	**36**	**IN**	**3 085**	**36**

property development around the course based on the American and European concept.

Barker conceived the idea of switching from dairy farming to golf course development after a visit to North America in the early 1980s to attend a Jersey cattle conference. While playing golf there he noted the American trend of building luxury homes on new course developments and decided that his farm in South Africa would be ideally suited for such a purpose. Barker had bought the Selborne Park estate from sugar magnate Vernon Crookes in 1978. It was Crookes who built the beautiful lodge in 1954 and had run the scenic estate as a Jersey stud farm. The land was ideal golfing terrain, although the hilly nature of the land meant that a number of up and down holes were inevitable.

Barker initially consulted a golf course architect but, after a lot of thought and research, decided to design the layout himself. For a layman, he has achieved an enviably high standard in creating his course. There are some controversial holes which could be improved upon, but the lasting impression is one of a tough challenge from start to finish. Magnificent homes have been built in the vicinity of the lodge and the clubhouse. Some of them overlook the green of the 4th hole, and the tee of the 5th, while others line the fairway of the 9th hole.

From the time the course was opened in 1987, Selborne Country Club has attracted interested

golfers from around the country. The Natal south coast is not short of golf courses, but Selborne is an upmarket venture of championship quality.

Played off the back tees, it is a strenuous test of golfing ability although it has not been host to a major tournament to date. It has a good mixture of long and short par-fours. The par-fives cannot be overwhelmed with power alone and the par-threes call for precise iron shots. Apart from the shotmaking, the greens are swift and sloping, and putting requires a deft touch.

The opening nine contain most of Selborne's feature holes. The 9th hole, an uphill par-four measuring 410 metres, would make an excellent finishing hole. The 18th hole, by comparison, is an attractive but not very demanding par-four where players can lay-up with a medium-iron off the tee to avoid any hazards.

The last nine holes, however, are by no means weak and during tournaments the players tend to attain better scores on the first nine holes than on the last nine.

ABOVE: *From the 6th green the championship tee can be seen, as well as the club tee across the bridge.*

OPPOSITE: *The 176-metre 15th hole features two dams in front of the green.*

Looking back towards the tee from the 8th green .

From the lodges on the hill, the 5th hole can be viewed across the green to the sloping fairway.

Selborne opens with two relatively gentle holes where making par can be straightforward if they are played conservatively. The 1st is a short dogleg par-five where there is a choice between laying-up off the tee or risking a tiger line over trees on the left, with an out-of-bounds fence lurking in wait for a hook. The 2nd is a short par-four, with a water hole to be avoided on the left. Water comes into play on 15 of the holes, although in many cases it punishes only the weak shots. The par-five 3rd is an outstanding hole and at 520 metres is the longest on the course, sweeping dramatically downhill to a green which is well guarded by water on three sides. There is an out-of-bounds fence on the left and tropical bush on the right. The safe option is to lay-up short with the second shot, but it is an exhilarating feeling to go for the green in two from the top of the hill.

The short 4th is intimidating with its sloping, two-tiered green set into the side of a hill. There is an extreme drop between the two tiers, and when the pin is on the bottom level the target is exceptionally small. Any shot falling short of the green will roll back into a water hole.

The par-four 5th hole runs downhill and a large water hazard laps the right-hand side of the sloping green, which lies in the valley below. The 6th is another par-three, with a pond in front of the green, and a variety of elevated tee positions make it play anything from a wedge to a long-iron. The par-four 7th is a dogleg-right, with an enormous flat green set on the crown of a hill; it plays longer than its 337 metres.

The 8th hole is only 290 metres long, but it is a marvellous example of a well-designed, short par-four. The tee shot has to carry a dam, then pass through a narrow passageway in the trees to reach the fairway beyond. Once that has been negotiated it is a relatively simple approach to an elevated, two-tiered green.

The 9th is a long, arduous, uphill par-four, and is justifiably the club's stroke-one hole. The tee shot has to be exact, to avoid a large tree on the left, and out-of-bounds on the right. A bunker guards the left front of the large green which is as much as three clubs' difference from front to back.

An attractive halfway house offers respite after the first nine holes, and the back nine is played in countryside that is more open, lacking the thick

The tricky, par-four 7th fairway features a large water hazard.

forest which hemmed in the fairways on the previous nine.

The 10th hole is a downhill par-five which looks generously wide off the tee, but narrows towards the green. A water hazard is strategically positioned to catch any overly long drives and has to be treated circumspectly.

The 11th hole is another par-three, reasonably short at 135 metres. Selecting the right club is important here as there is a dam behind the green, and the tee shot has to carry bush to reach the front edge of the green.

The tee of the par-five 12th, a sharp dogleg-left, is situated on one of the highest and most exposed parts of the course, and the drive has to carry tall trees and bush to reach the fairway below. From the fairway it is a steep climb to the green, and the hole plays longer than its 500 metres.

The 13th hole is a long par-four, again a dogleg-left. The 315-metre, par-four 14th is an unusual hole where the sensible ploy is to lay-up with an iron off the tee and then play the approach shot through the narrow avenue of trees leading to the green. The short 15th hole has two ponds at the front of the green, but there is lots of room to bail out on the sides, so it pays to take an extra club to avoid misfortune.

The 16th and 17th holes are both strong par-fours but, unfortunately, the same cannot be said of the tree-lined 18th which is short, narrow and overhung with branches. It is cluttered with an assortment of features and after playing 17 impressive holes, some golfers find it a disappointing end to the round. However, the spectacular view of the lodge behind the green makes one forgive this minor drawback.

WILD COAST SUN COUNTRY CLUB

Designed by Robert Trent Jones Junior

Robert Trent Jones Junior has designed the Wild Coast Sun Country Club course on one of the most beautiful and rugged coastlines of the world – an exciting visual experience and something quite unusual in South Africa. The famous American golf course architect has built 18 holes that are thoroughly modern in design, in this spectacular setting next to the Indian Ocean.

The Trent Jones signature lends a special aura to any club. It is probably the most famous and influential name in golf course architecture, attached to thousands of courses around the world, whether original or remodelled designs. Robert Trent Jones has been involved in course design since 1930 and it was not surprising that both his sons, Robert Trent Jones Junior and Rees Jones, joined the business. Robert joined his father's golf design firm in 1960, but in the 1970s left to form his own company. He has long advocated the concept of golf courses as works of art, blended with the environment, and this is evident at the Wild Coast layout. It is also the only Trent Jones Junior design in Africa. His father's name is only attached to one course in Africa, the Royal Dar es Salaam in Rabat, Morocco.

Simply riding a golf cart around the course at the Wild Coast Sun Country Club is an exciting and worthwhile experience, with its climbs and descents through ravines and across waterfalls, and breathtaking views of the sea and the undulating Transkei countryside. Virtually every hole is

The 17th green, positioned high on a hill, with the 18th fairway leading back towards the clubhouse.

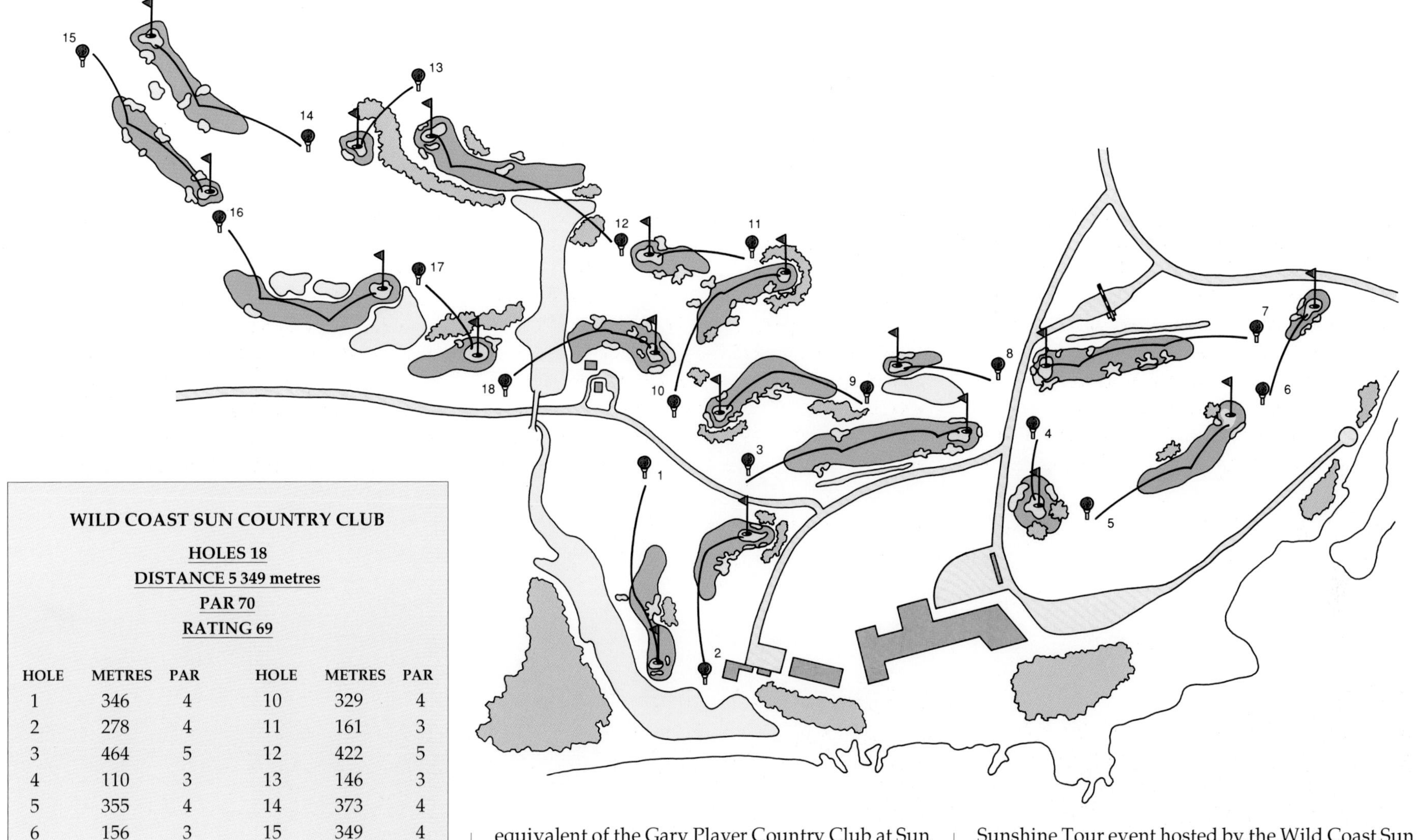

WILD COAST SUN COUNTRY CLUB

HOLES 18
DISTANCE 5 349 metres
PAR 70
RATING 69

HOLE	METRES	PAR	HOLE	METRES	PAR
1	346	4	10	329	4
2	278	4	11	161	3
3	464	5	12	422	5
4	110	3	13	146	3
5	355	4	14	373	4
6	156	3	15	349	4
7	465	5	16	460	5
8	138	3	17	145	3
9	325	4	18	327	4
OUT	**2 637**	**35**	**IN**	**2 712**	**35**

played in its own separate parcel of land, offering very little warning of the changing topography to come. Trent Jones has stretched his imagination to the full in sculpting a course from this rolling landscape. The layout is spread over such an extensive area of land that at times a golf cart seems advisable, even in a country where golfers prefer to walk and golf carts are a novelty. An alternative is to employ one of the Xhosa woman caddies, one of the original features of this club.

The Wild Coast Sun Country Club course was opened for play in 1983 as part of the large holiday resort complex and casino, ostensibly the coastal equivalent of the Gary Player Country Club at Sun City. No expense was spared in their respective designs, yet the two courses are totally unalike. Whereas the Gary Player Country Club course is long and punishing, the Wild Coast course is relatively short at under 6 000 metres off the championship tees. However, it is fraught with difficulty every step of the way.

On a calm day the Wild Coast is a paradise and the par of 70 seems simple enough, but when the wind is blowing, as it often does along this coast, the course can be a terrifying experience.

The difference in scoring can be illustrated by one of Mark McNulty's three victorious Sunshine Tour tournaments held at the Wild Coast. He had two rounds of 66 and 64 there during the November 1986 tournament, but sandwiched in between these scores were rounds of 75 and 74 played in the wind. McNulty's winning total on that occasion was one-under-par 279. A year later, at the last Sunshine Tour event hosted by the Wild Coast Sun Country Club, Tony Johnstone enjoyed a week of perfect conditions and was 17 shots better with a total of 262.

Before playing the Wild Coast course for the first time, it is advisable either to drive around the course in a cart or obtain some inside information to acquaint oneself with its hidden difficulties.

The 1st hole, for instance, sweeps down a steep hill to Thomson's Lagoon, with its green lying at the lowest point of the course. It generally requires only an iron from the tee; a shot played with a wooden club is in danger of running out of fairway. But for some golfers it is more exciting to confront each new hole as it arises and savour the unpredictability of the course.

The land lends itself to more par-threes than is usually the norm, and Trent Jones has not stayed within the convention of having four – the Wild Coast course features six par-three holes. The 4th

hole is extremely short at 110 metres off the back tee, but missing the green is fatal. This hole has been compared to the celebrated Postage Stamp hole at Royal Troon in Scotland.

At the 6th, another par-three, you hit from a high tee to the green below, with a view of the Umtamvuna River and its bridge which forms the border between Natal and the Transkei. The 8th hole, a 169-metre par-three, has a large pond on the left of the green. The 11th hole is slightly longer, measuring 188 metres, and being one of the highest points on the course is exposed to the wind, while also having a tricky sloping green to negotiate.

The 13th hole allowed Trent Jones to bring a natural waterfall into play, and this is a fearsome par-three with a yawning chasm to be carried to a wide green which is partly concealed by rocks and bush. In the first Sunshine Circuit tournament held there in 1984, when Severiano Ballesteros was the guest celebrity, McNulty holed a birdie putt on the

ABOVE: *The par-three 6th hole overlooks the Umtamvuna River and its bridge, which form the border between Natal and the Transkei.*

OPPOSITE: *The 8th green: this course, carved out of the rugged Transkei countryside, makes full use of the naturally undulating land.*

The green of the short 4th hole affords a spectacular view of the Indian Ocean.

WILD COAST CLASSIC WINNERS

1984	Mark McNulty (276)
1985	Ian Palmer (277)
1986	(February) Mark McNulty (267)
1986	(November) Mark McNulty (279)
1987	Tony Johnstone (262)

WILD COAST SKINS WINNERS

1987	Curtis Strange ($160 000)
1988	Chip Beck ($180 000)
1989	Scott Hoch ($350 000)
1990	José-Maria Olazábal ($160 000)
1991	Fred Couples ($180 000)
1992	Ian Woosnam ($170 000)

13th green which travelled from one side to the other, a distance of 35 metres. The 17th is the last of the short holes.

Anyone who plays the Wild Coast Sun Country Club course will cherish the memory of the 12th hole, a spectacular par-five. On leaving the 11th green you walk to the edge of a high cliff and down

One of the most breathtaking holes on the course, the par-five 12th hole is played through a valley to the elevated green.

in the valley below is a ribbon of fairway threading its way past a stream which has bush hugging its banks. It is only 441 metres in length, but from such a height it appears much longer. There are few feelings more exhilarating than when launching a solidly struck tee shot off the 12th tee and watching the ball plummet into the valley below. A long tee shot played to the left, although flirting with danger, can be rewarding as the elevated green is then in sight and within reach of a second shot. From the 12th green there is a railway car to transport golfers out of the valley to the 13th tee on the plateau above.

Water presents a major hazard on the closing stretch. The par-five 16th hole has a series of lakes to avoid, while the 18th requires a long carry over a large, man-made dam from the back tee. Again, the hole looks longer than it is. The opulent clubhouse stands on a hill overlooking the 18th hole.

A combination of exciting golf and resplendent countryside makes the Wild Coast Sun Country Club an essential stop on any golfing holiday.

A funicular railway takes golfers from the 12th green, which is in a valley, to the 13th tee on the plateau above.

The 8th hole exhibits the perfectly manicured but demanding features typical of the Wild Coast Sun course.

FISH RIVER SUN COUNTRY CLUB

Designed by Gary Player

Building a golf course along this windy stretch of Eastern Cape coastline in the vicinity of the Fish River proved one of the most challenging and frustrating projects ever undertaken by Gary Player and his team of course designers in South Africa. The site was perfect for construction purposes, but interminably dry, windy weather meant that it took close to two years for the course to reach a satisfactory condition for play.

Player had his first look at the rough layout in November 1988, when he walked the course and gave his final approval to the design. Eighteen months passed before he returned to hit the first tee shot at the official opening of the course in 1990.

The difficulties arose after the 18 holes had been carved out of the rugged, indigenous bush to complement the Polynesian-style architecture of the new Fish River Sun hotel and casino. The intention of having bent-grass greens, similar to those at the Gary Player Country Club in Sun City and the Wild Coast Sun Country Club, had to be discarded as the tiny grass seeds were blown to all corners of the Ciskei countryside by repeated gale-force winds before they could germinate.

Although Player was adamant when he first saw the course that he could succeed in growing Pentcross bent-grass greens, he had to comply with the

The 1st green affords a spectacular view of the ocean and the first nine holes laid out in the valley below.

vagaries of the local weather. Eventually bayview grass, which had previously been planted at the Humewood links in Port Elizabeth, was substituted for the bent grass, providing an equally good putting surface.

To compound the problem, a drought in the area meant that watering the new fairways, tees and greens was more difficult than had been anticipated. A new dam had to be built, together with

FISH RIVER SUN COUNTRY CLUB

HOLES 18
DISTANCE 6288 metres
PAR 72
RATING 73

HOLE	METRES	PAR	HOLE	METRES	PAR
1	365	4	10	345	4
2	170	3	11	479	5
3	495	5	12	383	4
4	388	4	13	178	3
5	371	4	14	525	5
6	183	3	15	406	4
7	472	5	16	360	4
8	338	4	17	174	3
9	337	4	18	373	4
OUT	**3 119**	**36**	**IN**	**3 169**	**36**

The green of the 3rd hole, lined with euphorbia trees, lies in view of the opulent hotel complex.

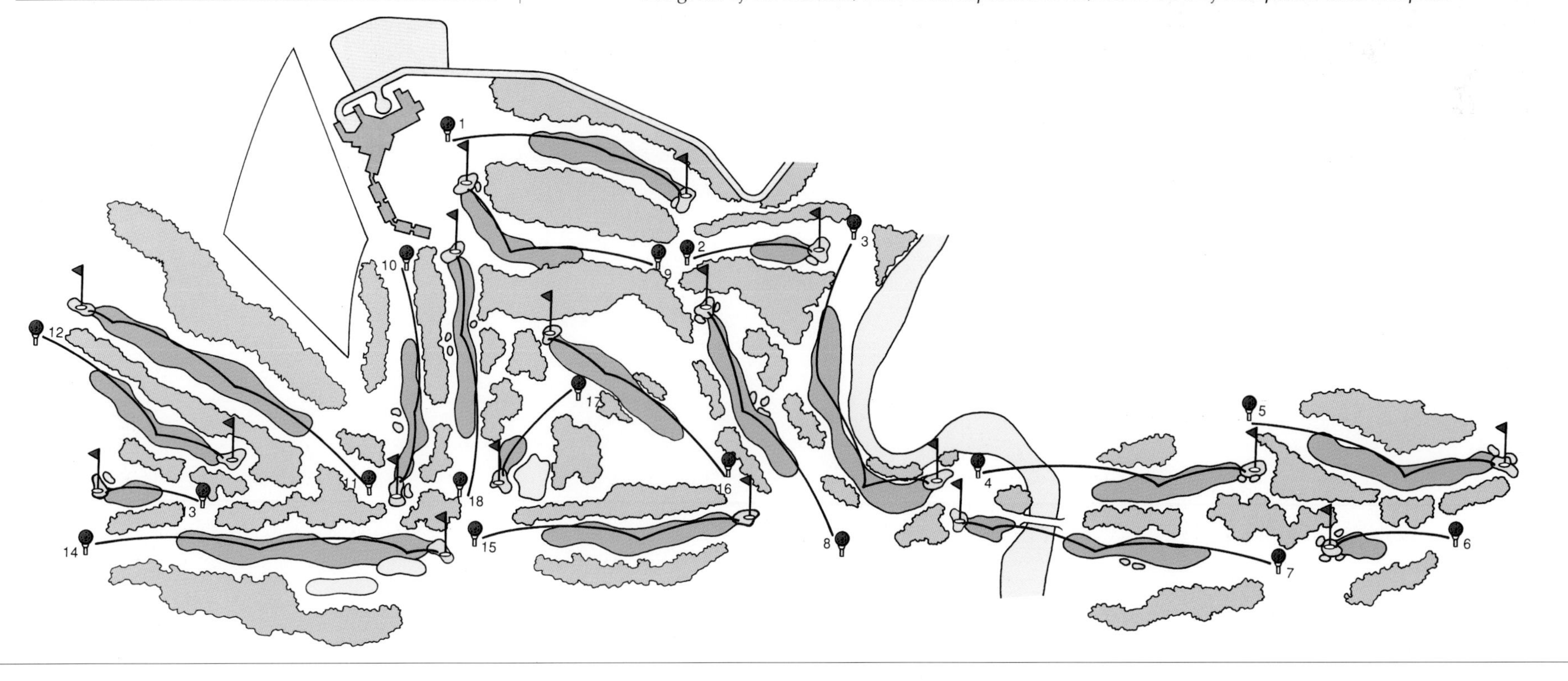

The fairway of the par-five 3rd hole curves to the left around a bend in the Old Woman's River. The bold player can attempt to carry the water with the second shot.

Pontoon Bridge crossing the Old Woman's River, which splits the first nine holes into two sections. In the background is the green of the par-five 7th.

FISH RIVER SUN CLASSIC WINNERS

1991	Derek James (285)

boreholes, to supplement the supply of water – a precious commodity in this dry region.

During the construction of the Fish River Sun course, which entailed bulldozing holes through the bush, Player took great care not to disturb the indigenous vegetation, especially the euphorbia trees which are common to this region. They stand like tall sentinels along several of the holes and apparently reminded Player of the huge cactus trees found on the desert courses in America.

Situated near Port Alfred, approximately an hour's drive from East London and two hours from Port Elizabeth, the course is located along the coast near the Fish River mouth. It does not, however, resemble a typical seaside course.

Being reasonably long, especially off the back tees, and having kikuyu fairways, it is best appreciated in the fine weather which is often experienced in the winter months, and not in the high winds that are known to blow in this area. Characteristic of a Player design, it has several memorable holes, each presenting a number of challenges.

The Old Woman's River splits the front nine holes into two sections, with four lying on the far side of the course from the hotel. A floating bridge has been built across the river, which is some 50 metres wide and has to be carried twice, first with the tee shot at the par-four 4th hole, and again at the par-five 7th hole.

The gently descending par-four opening hole affords a grand view of the ocean and the front nine holes laid out in the valley below.

The scenic par-five 3rd hole, a highly original creation measuring 495 metres from the back tee, is one of the most exciting holes on the Fish River Sun golf course. The fairway curves to the left and around a bend in the river. The challenge of this hole lies in the boldness of the person playing it, as it can be played conservatively, away from the river, for a reasonably safe score of five. However, if the wind is favourable a brave second shot can be attempted across a corner of the river to the green which is perched on a high bank, partially concealed by the rough vegetation.

To reach the 7th green, the Old Woman's River has to be safely carried and the strategically placed bunker avoided.

Another striking hole forming part of the front nine is the 5th hole, a medium-length par-four of 358 metres, which doglegs to the left. This is one of the few greens presenting a small target, and the trees in the middle of the greenside bunkers are an unusual feature.

The 472-metre 7th hole presents another tough poser. Unless the westerly wind is blowing towards you, the dilemma arises whether to attempt a risky second shot with a wooden club to carry the river, or lay-up short and then face a long third to the extensive, undulating green. Scoring a five at this hole can be a most satisfying experience. Although it is set near the mouth of the river, the Indian Ocean is to an extent hidden along this lower part of the course by high dunes. The sea and the beach can really only be seen from the loftier position of the hotel.

The front nine finishes with two relatively short but tricky par-four holes which climb back uphill towards the hotel.

The back nine comprises an interesting variety of testing holes, all twisting in various directions, making the wind an ever-changing factor. The 11th hole, measuring 462 metres, is an excellent par-five, with its fairway tightly guarded by bush as it curves first to the left and then right.

ABOVE: *The par-four 18th hole is played uphill towards the hotel, bringing the ocean back into view from the 18th green.*

OPPOSITE: *The tee shot at the 4th hole has to carry the river to the fairway on the opposite bank.*

Gary Player prefers his designs to include some long holes and at the Fish River these can be found in the stretch from the 13th to the 15th holes. The par-three 13th and par-five 14th are fairly straightforward, but the par-four 15th hole, with a fairway which initially threads its way through thick bush and then curves left, has character as well as being a demanding two-shotter to a sloping green.

Of all of the short holes the 17th is the most interesting, with its green built at the edge of a dam. When the hole is cut on the left, close to the water, it makes for an intimidating tee shot. After that, the final hole is played uphill to the hotel.

Despite the problems faced in building this course, all the hard work has proved worthwhile as the Fish River brings another championship course to the Eastern Cape; one that is set to gain considerable respect and prestige in the years to come, having already hosted tournaments on the South African Winter Tour.

EAST LONDON GOLF CLUB

Designed by George Peck

The many steep climbs encountered while playing this undulating golf course, which is perched in isolation on prime land next to the sea, leave one breathless – as do the striking views of the Indian Ocean and the city's beachfront.

'East Bank', as the 18 holes at the East London Golf Club are known locally, is one of the several unusual and rugged courses found in the Eastern Cape. Situated close to the centre of this port on the Buffalo River, the course leads one into a world of roller-coaster golf. It is an exciting experience to play East London for the first time, as it produces so many unexpected delights over its generously diverse area.

From the elevated clubhouse, which offers a magnificent outlook over the sea and sandy beaches, it is hard to form any kind of picture of the course itself. Most of it is concealed in the hills and dense bush from which the course was carved, an undertaking of demanding proportions when laid out in 1923 by professional golfer George Peck at a cost of £5 500. The course was remodelled later in the 1920s by Colonel S.V. Hotchkin, who designed Humewood and was associated with improve-

An aerial view of the course, showing the hilly terrain and its proximity to the Indian Ocean.

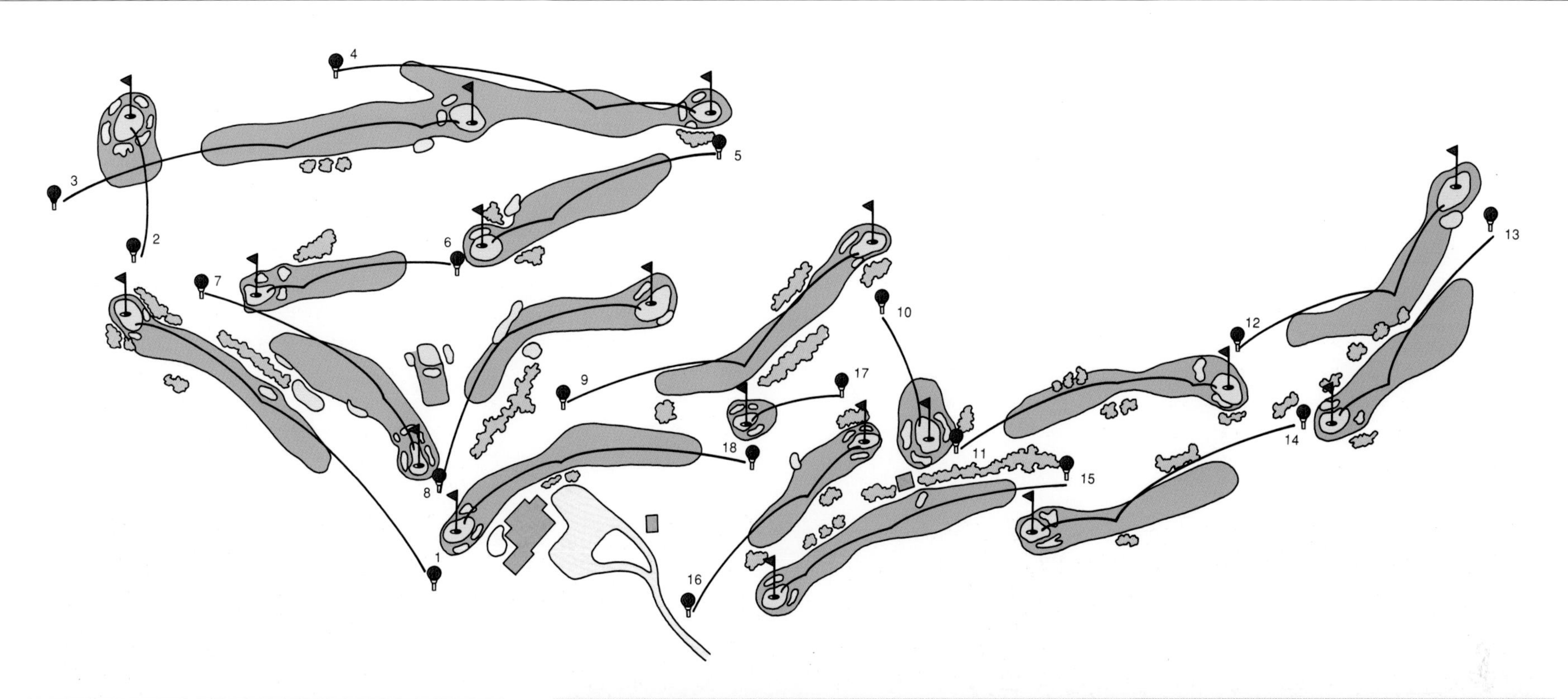

EAST LONDON GOLF CLUB

HOLES 18
DISTANCE 6038 metres
PAR 73
RATING

HOLE	METRES	PAR	HOLE	METRES	PAR
1	425	5	10	166	3
2	161	3	11	462	5
3	450	5	12	392	4
4	330	4	13	301	4
5	267	4	14	397	4
6	282	4	15	472	5
7	340	4	16	292	4
8	350	4	17	150	3
9	425	4	18	376	4
OUT	**3 030**	**37**	**IN**	**3 008**	**36**

ments at Maccauvlei Golf Club and Durban Country Club.

It took great foresight and imagination to build a course on this hilly ground when more practical sites were available elsewhere, but it was the club's third move and this time they were determined to acquire land in an inaccessible area where they would not easily be moved by the municipality.

The 1st green is in view of the elevated clubhouse.

The club itself came into existence in 1893 and is one of the oldest in the country.

To some extent the Eastern Cape led the way in the development of golf in South Africa: between 1889 and 1892 clubs had also been formed at Dordrecht, Port Elizabeth, Uitenhage, King William's Town, Adelaide and Bedford.

The present East London course has been host to six South African Open championships; the first won by Sid Brews in 1930, and the last by Gary Player in 1967. The only reason East London is no longer part of the Open roster is that South Africa's premier golfing event is now restricted to the three major centres: Johannesburg, Cape Town and Dur-

ABOVE: *Reached by a tee shot that is played across a valley, the sloping 9th fairway follows another valley to the green.*

OPPOSITE: *There is a magnificent sea view from the green of the short, par-four 5th hole.*

The 340-metre, par-four 7th hole is played from an elevated tee to a sloping fairway.

ban. The club, however, is a popular venue for South African Golf Union events and has staged numerous South African Amateur championships and interprovincial events.

Although it lies close to the sea, East London Golf Club cannot really be regarded as seaside golf of the variety provided at Humewood or Milnerton. Its rolling, bushy confines are similar rather to parts of Durban Country Club. Wind is always a factor and can tear through the valleys with tremendous force. At just over 6 000 metres from the back tees the course is not particularly long, but its strength lies in the numerous dogleg holes and the well-guarded, sloping greens.

The 425-metre 1st hole is a par-five which climbs gently uphill and gives no clue as to what lies ahead. It is followed by the first of many steep walks from green to tee as well as the first of the glorious views. The 2nd hole is a par-three which drops precipitously from tee to green. This type of hole was evidently popular among early South African course architects as several courses had par-threes of the pulpit variety, with sheer drops to the green, or the Majuba version where the green towers above the golfer.

East London has a strong starting stretch, with the only relatively weak holes on the front nine being the two back-to-back, short par-fours: the 5th and 6th. Through the years, club members have pondered over alternative designs for this section, but happily have not altered them to date as they are delightful holes to play. They are short enough for players to drive the greens with a tailwind, but trouble lies in wait for any shot not played straight.

When playing the uphill 5th hole with its blind tee shot, lungs bursting from the exertion of climbing the steep hill, pause at the top and take in the panoramic sea view looking back over the hole. It is hard to match and makes the climb seem that much more worthwhile.

After this interlude the course firms up again. The par-four 7th is played from a high tee to a

SOUTH AFRICAN OPEN WINNERS

1930	Sid Brews (297)
1937	Bobby Locke (288)
1948	Mickey Janks (298)*
1954	Reg Taylor (289)
1961	Retief Waltman (289)
1967	Gary Player (279)

* Won play-off against Sandy Guthrie

SOUTH AFRICAN AMATEUR WINNERS

1920	Bernard Wynne
1937	Bobby Locke
1948	Ben Ryan
1954	Alan Jackson
1961	Jannie le Roux
1972	Neville Sundelson
1982	Neil James
1986	Ernie Els

SOUTH AFRICAN STROKE PLAY WINNERS

1972	Phil Dunne (292)
1982	Wen-Shen Li (290)
1986	Ching-Sen Hsieh (289)

Looking down on the 2nd green from its high tee.

sloping fairway, and the 8th is a dogleg-right where the approach shot has to be played to a tricky, two-tiered green.

A walk along a sandy path through thick bush brings one to the best hole on the course, the 9th, once a par-five, now an intimidating yet spectacular par-four. The tee shot is played across a valley to a steeply sloping fairway that plunges down the other side of the hill into another valley. This hole doglegs left, and a long-hitter able to shape a draw around the corner of the dogleg can gain a big advantage. At the far end of the valley the long, narrow green presents a difficult target.

The par-three 10th must be played before the tea hut comes into sight. This is an awkward hole as the tee shot is played through a protected chute towards a green exposed to cross-winds.

The 11th is another dogleg-right, this time a par-five with big trees on the right penalizing any drive that is not kept to the left. The par-four 12th is one of the feature holes on this course. The fairway dips into a deep depression short of the green, which is tucked between sand dunes. At the back of the green there is a sheer drop to the beach below.

The 13th provides breathing space before the tough, par-four 14th, where a gradual climb to the flat green makes the hole play longer than its 397 metres. The 15th is a reasonably straightforward par-five, the tee shot having to be played to the crest of a hill, and the 16th is an attractive short par-four. The 17th is the third and last of the club's par-threes, and again features an elevated tee shot across bush to a well-protected green.

The 18th is an unusual finishing hole, with a sharp dogleg-left. The tee shot is tight, with the drive having to be threaded through a valley to a narrow fairway. Trees and bush line the hole on both sides, and an out-of-bounds appears on the left. A good drive plummets down a hill on the other side, and the second shot to a big green usually has to be played from a downhill lie or from the side of the hill. The clubhouse stands high on a ridge left of the fairway. Legends abound of long-hitters who, with the wind behind them, have gone for the green off the tee, striking their drives over the clubhouse roof.

Several improvements have been made to the course in recent years and are an indication of the club's willingness to modernize. The thick bush which lined the fairways and saw any wayward shots irretrievably lost has been thinned out, and a water reticulation system has been installed, making the course more lush, as well as making it play longer than previously.

FANCOURT COUNTRY CLUB

Designed by Gary Player

Gary Player's recently created golf course at Fancourt, near George on the picturesque Garden Route, has been received with acclaim since its opening in 1991. Fancourt, which is being transformed into an exclusive golfing estate on a par with those in the United States and Europe, has generated enormous interest both in South Africa and overseas. Player has designed 27 magnificent holes at this luxury estate, which is positioned in splendour next to the slopes of the Outeniqua Mountain range, and the course has already taken its place among the finest in the country.

The Outeniqua Mountains were responsible for bringing the Englishman Henry Fancourt White to South Africa in the 1840s. A road engineer, he built the famed old Montagu Pass through the mountains linking George to the Karoo. The original road is still there for tourists to explore. White loved the area, and in 1859 he built Fancourt House. He died a poor man in 1866, having lost all of his wealth in the economic depression of 1860. The house had several owners thereafter, until it was restored in the 1960s by the world-renowned brain surgeon Dr Roland Anthony Krynauw. Fan-

The luxuriously appointed Fancourt clubhouse, set against the Outeniqua Mountains.

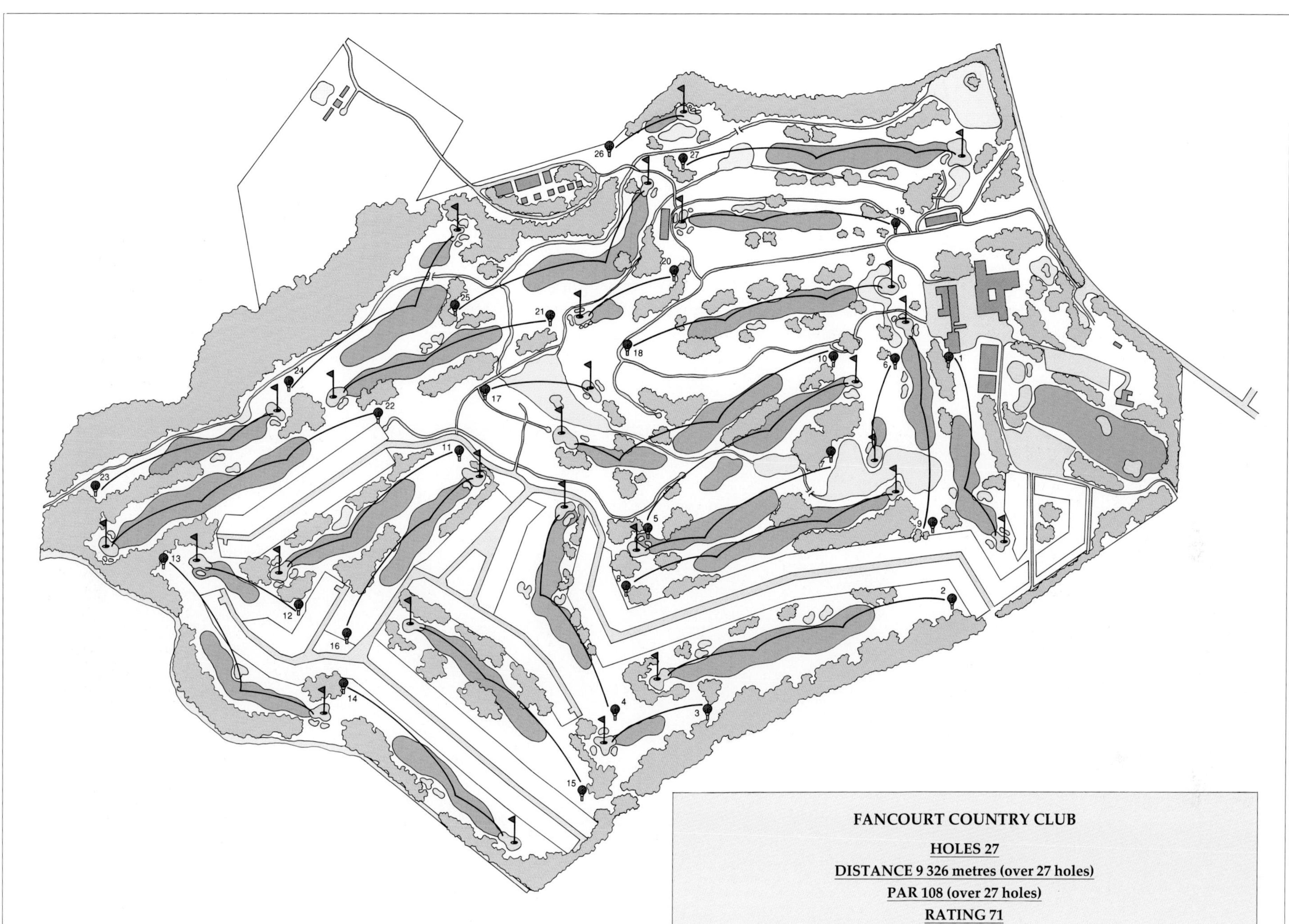

court was then acquired by movie magnate André Pieterse and his wife Helena in 1969, and in 1987 they conceived the idea of converting the house into a hotel and turning the large property into a golfing estate.

Less than a year after opening, the course held the Hall of Fame Championship on the Sunshine Tour in December 1991, and the professionals were effusive in praising the quality of the greens. For a course that was still relatively new, the modern, contoured greens were exceptionally good, and they will continue to be an outstanding feature of this layout.

Fancourt has a definite air of exclusivity, and is a very private club. The course is not open to casual visitors, and entry is limited to those who own

FANCOURT COUNTRY CLUB

HOLES 27

DISTANCE 9 326 metres (over 27 holes)

PAR 108 (over 27 holes)

RATING 71

HOLE	METRES	PAR	HOLE	METRES	PAR	HOLE	METRES	PAR
1	315	4	10	480	5	19	337	4
2	497	5	11	354	4	20	170	3
3	170	3	12	172	3	21	398	4
4	358	4	13	398	4	22	486	5
5	420	4	14	380	4	23	325	4
6	149	3	15	377	4	24	370	4
7	395	4	16	319	4	25	399	4
8	470	5	17	182	3	26	138	3
9	343	4	18	450	5	27	474	5
IN/OUT 3 117		36	IN/OUT 3 112		36	IN/OUT 3 097		36

The 14th green: the greens at Fancourt are an outstanding feature of this club.

lodges on the estate, their guests, and visitors staying at the Fancourt Hotel.

The first 18 holes, built in open farmland, were completed in 1991, and the third nine holes were finished in early 1992. These new holes are the most memorable feature of the estate, being built in a river valley at a lower level than the rest of the course, and they will prove the most popular with golfers who enjoy a challenge.

OPPOSITE: *The tranquil 17th hole, a par-three measuring 182 metres, viewed here in the early morning mists.*

The trees and vegetation are already in place, and the holes have an aura of Augusta National about them as they snake through the valley. It is no secret that Player was asked to try and recreate some of the beauty of Augusta at Fancourt, and the par-three 17th hole is a replica of the famous 12th hole at the home of the United States Masters. The difference between them is that Fancourt's 17th has water virtually from tee to green, and plays a couple of clubs longer at 182 metres from the back tees. Attractive flowerbeds frame the green, lending a vivid splash of colour to this signature hole.

Thousands of new trees have been planted, and eventually Fancourt will develop into a beautifully wooded parkland layout. The rolling terrain provides a considerable variety of holes and several of the drives are played from elevated tee positions. Player has used the land to its best advantage in laying out the course. There are different tees on each hole to test every golfer, from the beginner to the scratch player.

The first 18 holes contain a good mixture of long and short par-fours. Two of these par-fours, the 1st and the 16th, are under 320 metres in length but they require precision approaches to set up a birdie chance on the sloping greens.

Two of the most striking holes on the course are the 13th and the 14th, both testing par-fours, built

The 480-metre, par-five 10th hole plays to a green bordered by bunkers and a water hazard.

between precipitous slopes running down to the Malgas River which borders the property. The 13th is a dogleg-left which tempts longer-hitters to carry a large bunker on the corner of the fairway, to lessen the length of the second shot. The 14th is a straight hole, but the sunken fairway presents a narrow target, framed by a steep bank on the left, bunkers on the right, and a severe drop to the river for any shot pushed too far to the right.

Three of the par-fives provide plenty of drama. The greens of the 8th (470 metres), 10th (480 metres) and 18th (450 metres) are within reach in two shots, but on each of them there is the risk of ending up in the water hazards which border the greens. The 18th is a particularly beautiful hole. The fairway runs through an avenue of mature oak trees, with lodges on either side, and water fronts the green in the shape of a horseshoe.

The toughest par-four is probably the 420-metre 5th hole. The hole plays from a high tee into a valley, with the fairway guarded on the right by a large water hazard. Wherever the ball lands, the approach to the green is all uphill. This green is again protected on the right, in this instance by large bunkers. This is followed by the 6th hole, an attractive and unusual par-three, where the green has been built on a spit of land which extends out into a large dam.

The third nine holes begin among the Fancourt lodges, with a shortish but difficult par-four where the tee shot has to be guided through a narrow gap between trees and the lodges. It is followed by the 20th hole, a spectacular par-three which is played from an elevated tee to a long and narrow green situated in the valley below. This is definitely a hole to be remembered.

HALL OF FAME CHAMPIONSHIP WINNER

1991 De Wet Basson (276)

The clubhouse overlooks the 9th green, which features a spectacular water hazard.

The 21st has a humpback fairway which, if cleared, gives a sight of the green on the other side. The 22nd is a reasonably straightforward par-five, with an elevated green. A cluster of deep bunkers hugs the left edge of the green. The 23rd hole is a gentle par-four, with an interesting green which ripples downwards from right to left in a series of gentle slopes.

The next two holes, both par-fours, are among the most challenging on the estate. The fairway of the 24th is guarded on the left by a stream, and has tall pine trees flanking the right edge. The second shot has to clear the stream, the green being tucked away in a leafy clearing on the opposite side.

A giant pine tree points the way on the 25th hole. It stands alone in the middle of the fairway on the corner of a sharp left-hand dogleg. It takes a good tee shot to reach the corner and have a clear view of the green. The stream is a constant hazard on the left. Steps lead up to the tee of the short 26th hole, a pretty par-three with a lily pond stretching down the right-hand side of the hole into the banks of the green, which curves in a slight L-shape towards the water. Bunkers guard the left side of the green, and this hole, while requiring only a short-iron, is fraught with danger.

Water hazards come into play again on the par-five 27th. There is a pond in front of the tee, and the stream crosses the fairway, moving along the right-hand side. The hole is long and straight and has an enormous green, protected by a large bunker in the middle front, and dams on either side.

Behind the green of the 18th hole stands the spectacular clubhouse, a luxurious building which compares with the best in the world. It features spikeproof carpets imported from the United States, which allow golfers to walk about as they please in their golf shoes. The Fancourt Hall of Fame, featuring plaques and photographs commemorating the great names in golf, from Bobby Jones to Seve Ballesteros, lines the wide corridor which runs the length of the clubhouse.

GEORGE GOLF CLUB

Designed by Dr Charles Molteno Murray

George Golf Club possesses one of the most beautiful, as well as one of the most fearsome, finishing holes in South Africa. Set against the Outeniqua mountains, the view while walking the rolling 18th hole towards the clubhouse is breathtaking. The mountains can be seen from every aspect of the course, but are particularly imposing from this hole, a scene which has been photographed time and time again, and one that leaves lasting memories for visitors to the club.

Golf was first played in George as far back as 1886, on a three-hole course which formed part of a private property, but it was another 20 years before George Golf Club was formed in 1906. Nine holes were laid out on the local common, but the club did not prosper because of a continual struggle against the heather, which grows prolifically in the area.

A new nine-hole course was built in the early 1920s. The area was cleared of heather and sand greens were built. A few years later they were replaced with grass greens, and a modest clubhouse was constructed. Between 1929 and 1931 the course was increased to 18 holes. The club called in

The clubhouse is in view of the tee on the par-three 17th hole.

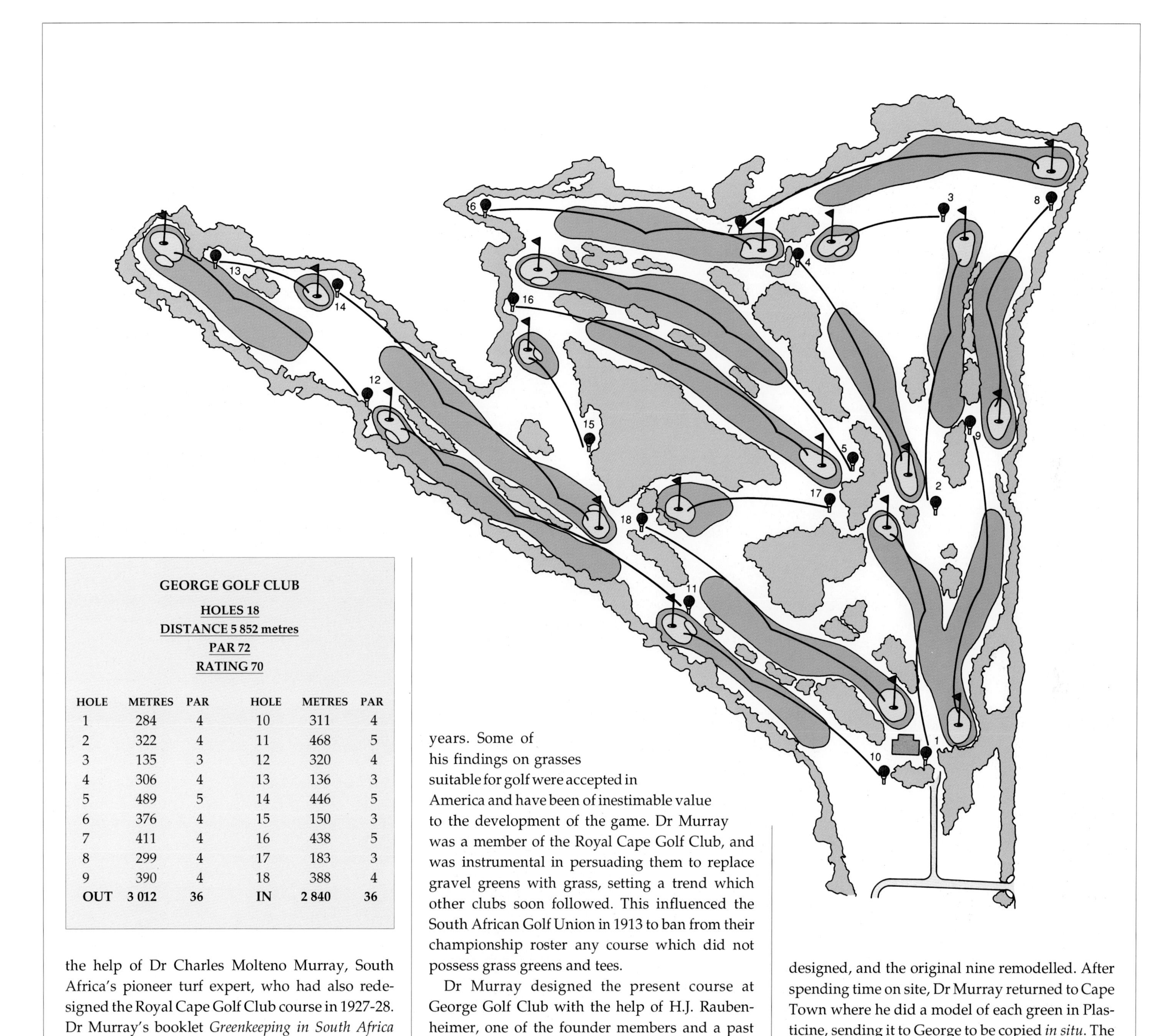

GEORGE GOLF CLUB

HOLES 18
DISTANCE 5 852 metres
PAR 72
RATING 70

HOLE	METRES	PAR	HOLE	METRES	PAR
1	284	4	10	311	4
2	322	4	11	468	5
3	135	3	12	320	4
4	306	4	13	136	3
5	489	5	14	446	5
6	376	4	15	150	3
7	411	4	16	438	5
8	299	4	17	183	3
9	390	4	18	388	4
OUT	**3 012**	**36**	**IN**	**2 840**	**36**

the help of Dr Charles Molteno Murray, South Africa's pioneer turf expert, who had also redesigned the Royal Cape Golf Club course in 1927-28. Dr Murray's booklet *Greenkeeping in South Africa* was the definitive work on the subject for many years. Some of his findings on grasses suitable for golf were accepted in America and have been of inestimable value to the development of the game. Dr Murray was a member of the Royal Cape Golf Club, and was instrumental in persuading them to replace gravel greens with grass, setting a trend which other clubs soon followed. This influenced the South African Golf Union in 1913 to ban from their championship roster any course which did not possess grass greens and tees.

Dr Murray designed the present course at George Golf Club with the help of H.J. Raubenheimer, one of the founder members and a past captain and president. Nine new holes had to be designed, and the original nine remodelled. After spending time on site, Dr Murray returned to Cape Town where he did a model of each green in Plasticine, sending it to George to be copied *in situ*. The Royal Cape Golf Club's centenary booklet, pub-

The tree-lined fairway leading to the green on the par-four 12th hole.

The 17th hole is one of the most outstanding par-threes in South Africa.

lished in 1985, says 'there is no better monument to Murray than the fine layout at George'.

The beauty of the course has developed over the years, with the growth of a variety of trees, and today it is an enchanting paradise, retaining a countrified air. The holes undulate through rolling valleys, and the golfer is required to display an assortment of shot-making skills during a round.

The short, relatively gentle opening holes can lull the golfer into a false sense of optimism. An iron can be used off the tee on each of the first four holes, the longest of which is 322 metres. It is quite easy to be under-par on the opening stretch, although anything off-line will be punished by the abundant trees, thick bush and heather lining the holes. The 1st, 2nd and 4th holes are all short par-fours while the par-three 3rd hole of 135 metres requires only a short-iron.

It is only from the par-five 5th hole, a long dogleg to the left, that the course starts showing its strength. This is followed by some extremely difficult holes, particularly the 7th and 9th.

The 411-metre, par-four 7th is one of the most attractive and daunting holes in the country, requiring two exceptionally good shots to reach a sloping green which has a steep drop to the left. The tee shot has to be played to the crown of a ridge, at which stage the fairway drops into a valley, leaving a long second shot to the green.

The fairway of the 390-metre 9th hole gives the impression of being a double dogleg. The tee shot is tight, skirting tall trees to a downhill fairway curving right, and which then moves left and slightly uphill to a large green.

The course is unusual in that there is only one par-three and one par-five on the front nine, while there are three of each on the back nine. The feature of both sets of nine holes is a gentle start which builds to a strong finish.

Slightly shorter than the first nine, the second half of the course also begins with a short par-four which is played to an elevated green. The par-five 11th is one of the club's character holes, with two large trees standing sentinel in front of the green. The approach shot must either be carried over the trees, or played to the left of them. An out-of-bounds fence borders the entire left-hand side of the fairway, and with the tee shot having to be kept left in order to approach the hole successfully, this

The 18th hole with its view of the Outeniqua mountains.

is a superb golf hole. The two remaining par-fives are the 14th and the 16th, and long tee shots can set up birdie opportunities on both of them.

Several of the greens on this latter nine are raised. Missing them carries a heavy price, as recovery is not easy from the bottom of the steep slopes.

The three short holes, the 13th, 15th and 17th, grow progressively more difficult. The tee shot on the 13th is uphill, while the other two are played from elevated tees. The 183-metre 17th is one of the most outstanding par-threes to be found anywhere in the country, and even from its high tee most golfers require a long-iron to reach the green which is wide, but quite shallow from front to back.

Having completed the 17th hole, the 388-metre, par-four finishing hole awaits. The fairway slopes from right to left, leaving the second shot to be played to a green which is positioned in a depression below the clubhouse. A large bush waits to trap any shot that strays to the right and is short. The new clubhouse, which was recently reconstructed around the old building, overlooks the 18th hole.

Between 1951 and 1963 George Golf Club was the permanent venue for the Cape Province Open amateur championship, which is now played there every fourth year.

Looking at the heavily wooded George Golf Club course today, with its incredible variety of trees, bushes and the famous George heather, it is hard to believe that when it was first constructed over eighty years ago, there was hardly a tree on the property. With plentiful rain in the area, however, there has been abundant growth, and playing a round of golf at George on a pleasant summer's day is very similar to a ramble through a private garden estate.

HUMEWOOD GOLF CLUB

Designed by Colonel S.V. Hotchkin

The late Bobby Locke once paid Humewood the ultimate compliment of suggesting that he would like to see the British Open played at this links. Situated in Port Elizabeth, on the windy Algoa Bay coast, Humewood Golf Club is similar to the top championship links in the British Isles. Its fairways are wider, however, as a concession to the strong winds that blow throughout the year – particularly from August to January – and it lacks the abundance of bunkers that accompany courses such as Muirfield and Royal Lytham.

During the peak of his career, Locke considered Humewood to be the finest course in South Africa, and he was not alone in his unstinting praise of what is generally regarded as English course architect Colonel S.V. Hotchkin's masterpiece.

Hotchkin first saw the site, which is located well away from the bustle of the city, in 1929, and the course was opened for play in 1931. Only in recent years has suburbia reached its borders but little of this is evident from the course, which has an abundance of wildlife. It is rugged golfing terrain with a bleak appearance on a windy day, yet it can be a picture of tranquillity on those rare occasions when

The clubhouse overlooks the green of the par-four finishing hole.

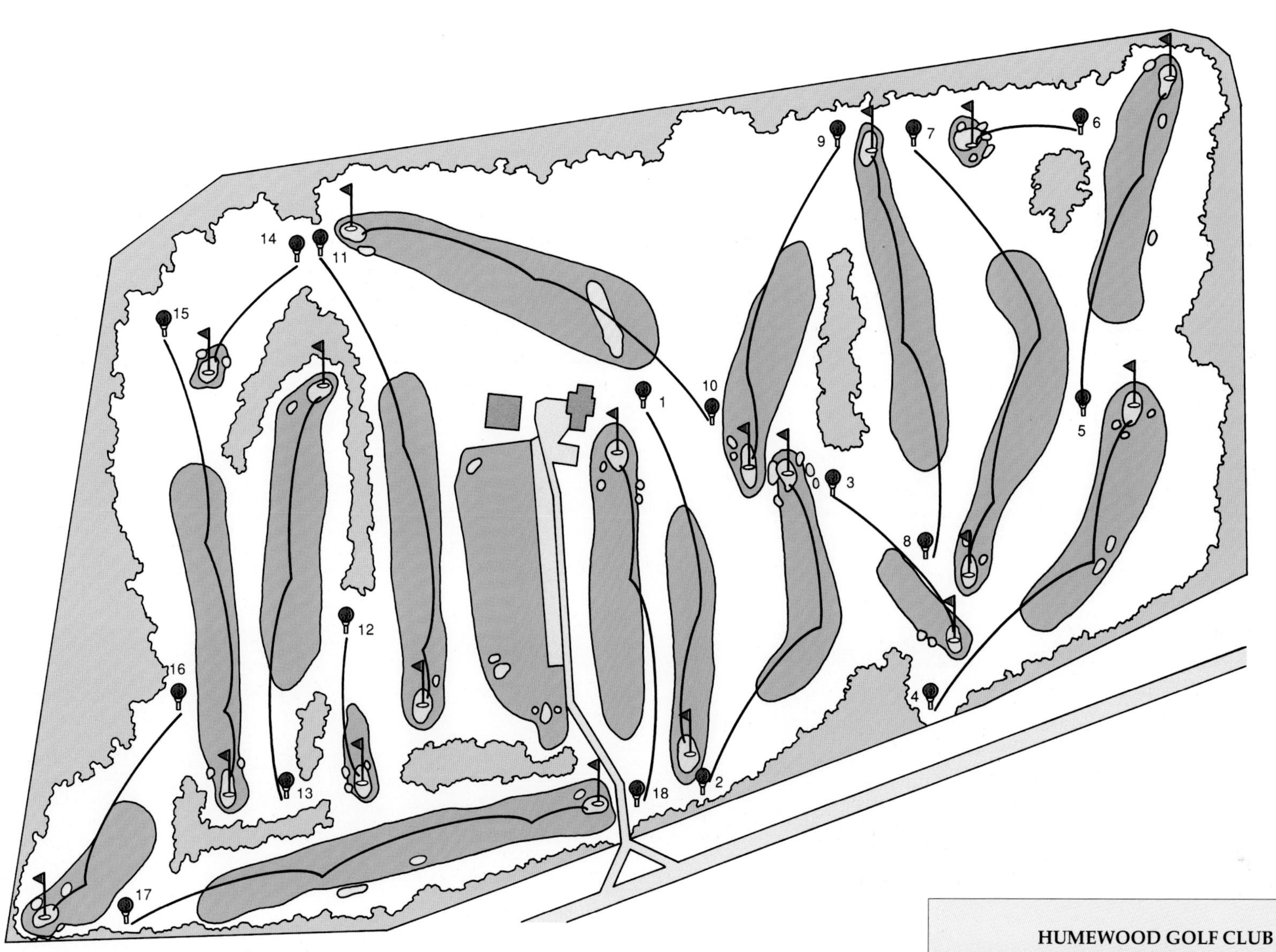

HUMEWOOD GOLF CLUB

HOLES 18
DISTANCE 6185 metres
PAR 72
RATING 72

HOLE	METRES	PAR	HOLE	METRES	PAR
1	357	4	10	420	4
2	361	4	11	477	5
3	198	3	12	154	3
4	394	4	13	409	4
5	338	4	14	145	3
6	128	3	15	456	5
7	475	5	16	271	4
8	414	4	17	495	5
9	329	4	18	364	4
OUT	**2 994**	**35**	**IN**	**3 191**	**37**

the air is still and Algoa Bay is as calm as a mill-pond. Hotchkin used the natural lie of the area, formerly sand dunes and thick bush, in designing this links and the rolling fairways with their mounds and hollows make for uneven lies on many of the holes.

The links was the concept of four Port Elizabeth Golf Club members, E.C. Hay, E. Allan, W.C. Marshall and professional Charles McIlvenny, who felt the need for another championship course in Port Elizabeth to take some of the pressure off the Port Elizabeth Golf Club. Within a few years of being completed it became a national championship venue, hosting both the South African Open and Amateur in 1934. The course remained part of the Port Elizabeth Golf Club, with members being able to choose between the two courses, until Humewood Golf Club took on its own identity in 1952.

Further Opens and Amateurs, which in that era were held at the same venue, were staged at Humewood in 1940, 1952 and 1957, with the final of the 1957 Amateur going to a record 41 holes, and a

From the green of the par-four 10th hole, looking back towards the tee.

The undulating fairway of the 13th, the most outstanding hole on the course.

SOUTH AFRICAN OPEN WINNERS

1934	Sid Brews (319)
1940	Bobby Locke (285)
1952	Sid Brews (305)
1957	Harold Henning (289)*

*Won 36-hole play-off against Sandy Guthrie

SOUTH AFRICAN AMATEUR WINNERS

1934	Clarence Olander
1940	Henry Watermeyer
1952	Mickey Janks
1957	Arthur Stewart
1965	Peter Vorster
1969	Deryck Thornton
1979	Louis Norval
1984	Mark Wiltshire

SOUTH AFRICAN STROKE PLAY WINNERS

1969	Dale Hayes (314)
1979	David Suddards (285)
1984	Derek James (287)

GOODYEAR CLASSIC WINNERS

1984	John Bland (277)*
1985	Denis Watson (282)
1986	Tony Johnstone (275)
1987	John Bland (281)
1988	Trevor Dodds (276)
1990	(February) Philip Jonas (287)
1990	(December) Fulton Allem (277)
1991	Justin Hobday (280)
1992	Ernie Els (276)

*Won play-off against Nick Price

36-hole play-off for the Open title. Although the club has continued to stage major amateur tournaments, the South African Open has not returned to Port Elizabeth since Harold Henning's victory in 1957, due to the South African Golf Union's policy of restricting the Open to the three major centres: Johannesburg, Cape Town and Durban.

Since 1984, Humewood has been the venue of the annual Goodyear Classic on the Sunshine Tour, where the winning scores have been among the highest recorded on the Tour.

A leading British golf course architect, Donald Steel, recently evaluated the links to ensure that it was up to date.

On entering Humewood, the long driveway winds past the 17th green and 18th fairway to the gracious, double-storey clubhouse which commands an impressive view of the exposed links and the Bay where the 1820 British Settlers first landed in South Africa.

The links originally had a club par of 76, with eight par-fives, but since the 1970s it has gradually been reduced to 72. Four of the par-fives are now extremely difficult par-fours. Par is a fickle thing at Humewood, however, and cannot be compared to that played in the benign weather conditions of the Transvaal. The wind can blow ferociously in Port Elizabeth, especially in the early summer months, and the par of a hole often depends on the direction of the wind. If the prevailing westerly is blowing, three of the par-fives on the links can be played as par-fours, as they can be reached in two shots. On the other hand, the long par-fours are into the wind and they become par-fives.

The 3rd hole, for instance, is a long par-three of 198 metres where a medium-iron is needed downwind, but a driver can be used if the wind shifts to an easterly direction.

The front nine is relatively flat, with several testing par-fours. The feature hole on this nine is the short 6th, a difficult par-three of 130 metres that is played in a cross-wind. This was the only green that needed building up during construction. It is narrow and elevated, guarded at the front and the sides by bunkers, and presents a difficult target in any conditions. Confronted by the 6th hole on a particularly windy day, Bobby Locke is said to have taken out his putter and run the ball along the path to the green.

The longer back nine encounters bigger sand dunes. The 13th is the most outstanding hole on the course, a 409-metre par-four which bears comparison with any of the great championship holes in the world. The fairway in the driving area is a corrugation of swales, and the green sits high on a sand dune with a large waste area of sand and rough catching any shot that is even the slightest bit pushed, and a cavernous bunker waiting for any shot that is pulled. It is played mainly into the prevailing westerly wind, so the second shot usually requires a wood or a long-iron.

The club's emblem is the crowned plover, a bird which inhabits the course and tends to nest on the fairways. Red flags are placed to mark these nests, and the local rule to protect the birds is that any ball lying within two club-lengths of a nest must be dropped away from it.

From the tee of the par-five 11th, looking out towards the sea.

The 6th hole, with its narrow green surrounded by bunkers.

MILNERTON GOLF CLUB

Designed by Archie Tosh

Nestled between the Atlantic Ocean and Table Mountain, Milnerton Golf Club possesses one of the most beautiful views of any golf course in South Africa – one that can change dramatically during a round of golf as the famous 'tablecloth' of cloud sweeps over the mountain. This vista can be distracting to the golfer, and it is probably for the best that the opening holes all face away from the mountain. It is particularly difficult to tear oneself away from the 3rd tee, perched only a few metres above the beach, with an outlook that compares with the best in the world. On a sunny day in Cape Town, with a light wind blowing, playing golf at Milnerton seems the only sensible thing to do.

The course itself is unusual by South African standards in that, being situated on a narrow stretch of land between a lagoon and the sea, it conforms to the traditional British links practice of nine holes out followed by nine holes back, rather than returning the 9th to the clubhouse, which is the norm of modern courses.

Milnerton Golf Club was conceived in 1925, and opened for play in the same year. Archie Tosh, the professional at the Metropolitan Golf Club in

The 12th hole, a difficult par-five, plays to an undulating, bunkered green.

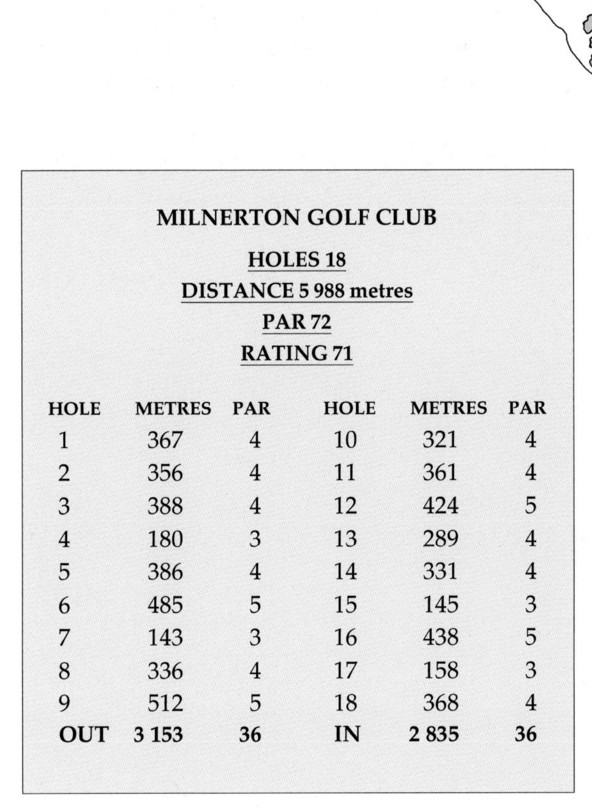

MILNERTON GOLF CLUB

HOLES 18
DISTANCE 5 988 metres
PAR 72
RATING 71

HOLE	METRES	PAR	HOLE	METRES	PAR
1	367	4	10	321	4
2	356	4	11	361	4
3	388	4	12	424	5
4	180	3	13	289	4
5	386	4	14	331	4
6	485	5	15	145	3
7	143	3	16	438	5
8	336	4	17	158	3
9	512	5	18	368	4
OUT	**3 153**	**36**	**IN**	**2 835**	**36**

Mouille Point, Cape Town, was engaged to assist in the layout of the course. On 1 May 1926, the Milnerton committee approved a motion to appoint Archie Tosh as the club's first professional. Tosh, a Scot, won the South African Open title in 1929 at Royal Cape Golf Club.

For many years the course struggled with a shortage of water, but the implementation of a water reticulation system has transformed it from a dry, patchy links to a lush, well-conditioned course. A modern clubhouse has been built next to the beach, and affords a magnificent view of the course, the sea and the mountains.

Milnerton is regarded by many golfers in Cape Town as a true links layout as it lies on sandy terrain. However, while the holes closest to the sea have links qualities, the adjacent holes are more parkland in nature. Furthermore, the fairways are flat rather than undulating and the course does not have the humps and hollows which are natural features of true links courses, created as they are from dunes bordering the sea. Nor does Milnerton possess the fearsome rough which is predominant in links golf, although there is plenty of bush lining the holes.

Even without the rough, Milnerton is an exacting test of shot-making, and when the wind blows even the most skilful player is confronted with a tough challenge. In such a situation it helps to be a strong long-iron player. The club staged the South African Masters tournament for several years on the Sunshine Tour, and it is an indication of the course's strength that the winners were among the finest golfers to come from southern Africa.

An outstanding feature of the course is its many sloping greens, reminiscent of championship layouts in Britain and the United States. The greens have improved considerably in recent years, after the introduction of the water reticulation system, and have a beautifully smooth texture, similar to that of bent grass (which was tried at Milnerton but discarded when it was burnt by the south-east wind during hot, windy summers). The slopes allow for some exciting pin positions.

Milnerton has a special appeal to golfers during the wet Cape winters, as the sandy base of the course allows it to drain well, making it playable at all times.

The direction of the wind determines the severity of the individual holes. When the south-easter blows, as it does regularly during the summer months, the opening nine are played mainly downwind. This may make the course appear easy, but once tea is taken at the halfway house, the nine

holes back to the clubhouse are played into the wind and this puts an entirely different perspective on matters. Looking at the card, the holes may not seem particularly long, but they are exceptionally difficult when played into a strong wind. The short par-four 13th, which can almost be driven from the tee, is the only hole protected from the wind.

The par-four 14th hole, measuring 331 metres, is a hole to be treated with respect. A dogleg-right, it requires an accurate tee shot followed by a long iron to find the well-bunkered green.

The closing holes also bring another hazard into play in the form of the lagoon which flanks the fairways to the left all the way back to the club-

ABOVE: *From the 3rd tee, the golfer is treated to a magnificent outlook over the sea to Table Mountain.*

OPPOSITE: *The short 15th hole, with its tree-lined fairway leading to a small, undulating green.*

The 17th tee: the lagoon poses a hazard to the left of this par-three.

Table Mountain changing colour as the sun sets creates a beautiful backdrop for the bunkered 15th green.

SOUTH AFRICAN MASTERS WINNERS

1978	Dale Hayes (275)*
1979	Gary Player (270)
1981	Nick Price (281)
1982	Mark McNulty (275)
1984	Tony Johnstone (277)
1985	Mark McNulty (278)

*Won play-off against Tienie Britz

house. Milnerton Golf Club has an unusual finish in that there are two par-threes, one par-four and one par-five from the 15th to the 18th holes. Both of the short holes, the 15th and the 17th, have tiny, undulating greens which are difficult to hit off the tee. The par-four 18th hole is a strong finishing hole, played to a green which is guarded by a water hazard and a bunker on the left. These closing holes create an appropriately exacting end to an enjoyable and challenging round of golf.

OPPOSITE: *The 5th is the club's stroke-one hole, a long par-four played to a large, sloping green.*

MOWBRAY GOLF CLUB

Designed by Robert Grimsdell and Charles Hugh Alison

Cape Town's older golf courses are graced with superb mountain views, and Mowbray Golf Club's 15th hole possesses one of the finest, almost diverting one's attention from the fact that two outstanding shots are required to reach the green. Mowbray is parkland golf, very English in its tree-lined setting, yet no English parkland course has as dramatic a backdrop as that provided by Devil's Peak. The 15th hole heads straight towards this majestic mountain.

The course has been the scene of numerous major tournaments over the last 60 years and has always defended itself well as a championship venue. There are six par-five holes on the card, although two of these are normally played as par-fours in professional tournaments to make a par of 72.

Mowbray Golf Club was founded in 1910, not far from Rondebosch Common where the Cape Golf Club (now Royal Cape Golf Club) had built their second course towards the end of the 19th century. When the Cape Golf Club moved for a second time, to its present site at Wynberg-Ottery, several of the members balked at the idea of travelling that distance and set to work acquiring Raapenberg Farm,

The 13th green, one of the greens recently improved by the addition of water hazards.

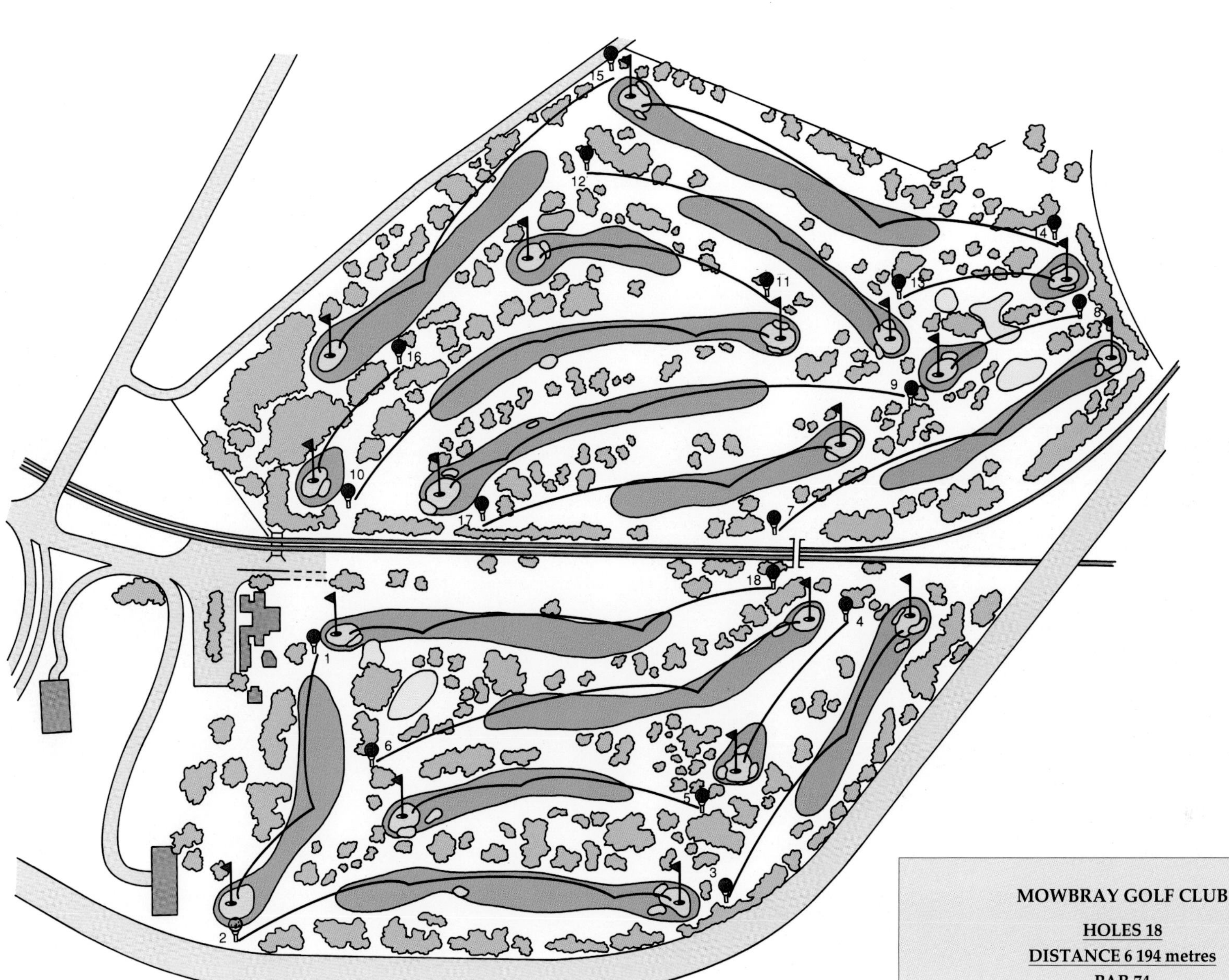

which they leased from the Mowbray municipal council, in order to construct their own course. One attraction of this area was that there was a railway station at Raapenberg.

The railway line still runs through the middle of the course, and is a busy suburban line. Former South African Open champion Gavin Levenson, playing in a Sunshine Tour event at Mowbray, studied the train timetables so that he knew when to expect their arrival and wouldn't be distracted while playing a shot.

As with so many of the championship courses in South Africa, Robert Grimsdell had an influence on Mowbray's design as it stands today. Grimsdell first came to South Africa from England at the age of 15, and fought for the South African forces in France during the First World War. Following the armistice, he took up an appointment as the professional at the Chorley Golf Club in Lancashire. It was there that he became attracted to golf course design and architecture through a friendship with Charles Hugh Alison of the respected firm of Colt

MOWBRAY GOLF CLUB

HOLES 18
DISTANCE 6 194 metres
PAR 74
RATING 72

HOLE	METRES	PAR	HOLE	METRES	PAR
1	316	4	10	482	5
2	445	5	11	293	4
3	341	4	12	352	4
4	180	3	13	176	3
5	321	4	14	465	5
6	441	5	15	392	4
7	382	4	16	153	3
8	169	3	17	366	4
9	474	5	18	446	5
OUT	**3 069**	**37**	**IN**	**3 125**	**37**

The 18th green, with its large water hazard, is played in view of the clubhouse.

and Alison. They were to become lifelong friends. Alison entered into golf course architecture in 1920, after meeting Harry Colt and subsequently going into partnership with him. He has a long list of courses around the world to his name including Glendower, Bryanston and Vereeniging in the Transvaal. Alison was regarded as probably the first truly international golf course architect, being credited with the design of courses in America, Europe, Japan and Australia.

Grimsdell did not stay away from South Africa for long and decided to make his home in Cape Town. He spent his early years as a professional at Mowbray in the 1920s. He accepted the position of professional at the Johannesburg Golf Club in 1926, however. He returned to Mowbray in 1932 to play in the first South African Open hosted by the club and finished second in that championship behind Charles McIlvenny. Twenty years later he was back again to modernize the course layout following the untimely death in 1952 of Alison, who had initially been commissioned to do the job.

The modernization of Mowbray Golf Club's course coincided with the introduction of the club's

SOUTH AFRICAN OPEN WINNERS

1932	Charles McIlvenny (304)
1947	Ronnie Glennie (293)
1960	Gary Player (280)
1971	Simon Hobday (276)
1975	Gary Player (278)
1978	Hugh Baiocchi (285)
1987	Mark McNulty (278)*

* Won play-off against Fulton Allem

SOUTH AFRICAN AMATEUR WINNERS

1932	Christian Watermeyer
1960	Murray Grindrod
1966	Comrie du Toit
1970	Hugh Baiocchi
1976	Russell Kotzen

SOUTH AFRICAN STROKE PLAY WINNERS

1970	Dale Hayes (291)
1976	George Harvey (276)*

* Won play-off against Peter Todt

BELL'S CUP WINNERS

1991	John Bland (277)
1992	David Feherty (276)
1993	Vijay Singh (278)

first water reticulation system in 1951, which allowed water to be pumped on to the course from the nearby Black River. Prior to the installation of this system, the club had fought a continuous battle to keep the grass alive during the arid, windy summers. The old 17th 'Railway Hole' at Mowbray was eliminated during the modernization and a number of new holes were built while others were altered considerably.

Grimsdell stepped in to complete the plans in the spirit of Alison's ideas and, over the years, continued to assist the club in updating holes.

This modernization policy has continued to the present day. After the 1987 South African Open was held at Mowbray, the club spent R1,6-million on the course and clubhouse, creating new water hazards and installing a new water reticulation scheme. The finishing hole had previously been a reasonably innocuous par-five where the top players reaped a large share of birdies, but the water hazard to the left of the green now makes this a far more difficult proposition.

After disdaining water hazards for many years, the club has introduced them as central features

At 180 metres, the 4th hole is the longest par-three on the course.

The 14th green, flanked by two large bunkers.

The contoured green of the par-four 11th hole.

between the 7th and 8th holes, as well as on the 11th and 13th holes.

Gary Player won two of his 13 South African Open titles at Mowbray, and almost claimed a third on this course, where he has played some of his finest rounds. In 1960 he made one of his typical last-round charges, finishing with a score of 66 which included seven birdies and two eagles to beat Harold Henning and Tommy Trevena.

The final round in 1971, however, provided one of the most dramatic and controversial days of golf in the history of the South African Open. Player started the last day of the tournament five shots behind Simon Hobday and had seven consecutive birdies from the 9th to the 15th holes – an incredible run – to go nine-under-par for the round.

Although Hobday was holding up well under pressure, Player, who had won his three previous tournaments, looked a certain winner when Hobday plugged his second shot into a bunker at the par-five 14th hole. The ball was buried so firmly in the sand that Hobday could not get it out of the bunker with his next shot and it rolled back towards him. Hobday scrambled out of the way but thought he felt something hit his foot. He couldn't be sure if it was the ball, although spectators insisted that it had not touched him. He recovered for a five and made par on his way back for a closing total of 69, to learn that Player had dropped shots at the 16th and 18th holes, scoring a 65 instead of a 63, and that he had finished one shot clear of Player. The South African Golf Union, however, deliberated whether Hobday should be penalized two shots for the incident in the bunker at the 14th hole. Had the ball touched him or not?

Hobday described the wait as the 'longest half-hour of my life' as the SAGU officials heard all the evidence, before they came out to pronounce him the new champion.

Mowbray today is not as thickly lined with trees as it was when Player was at the height of his success, many of them having died through disease, but it still retains a parkland look.

Teeing off from in front of the clubhouse, the 316-metre 1st hole provides an easy start, a short par-four between tall trees with the fairway curving right and downhill to a green which can be reached with the tee shot in the right conditions. The 2nd is a straightforward par-five, although the green is well bunkered, and is followed by the 3rd, another shortish par-four.

The 4th is the longest par-three on the course at 180 metres, and the flat green makes for a decidedly difficult hole. The 5th is extremely picturesque, framed by trees and mountains. It is also relatively short, with a slight dogleg-left off the tee.

At this point the course becomes more difficult, with the 6th being a long, testing hole swinging left around a stand of trees. The 7th is a medium par-four, and the par-three 8th is one of the holes improved by the addition of a water hazard.

The 9th and 10th holes are back-to-back par-fives, the green of the 474-metre 9th hole being closely protected by trees on the left. The 482-metre 10th takes a dogleg-right on the corner of the driving area. The 11th hole, a par-four measuring only 293 metres, has been strengthened by the addition of a large water hazard on the right of the green.

The par-four 12th, the par-three 13th which features another water hazard, and the par-four 14th are fairly straightforward holes, leading up to the famous 15th hole. Measuring 392 metres, this par-four runs through an avenue of pine trees directly towards Devil's Peak. Nearing the green, the fairway suddenly becomes severely undulating, hiding the green from sight.

Played back towards the railway line, the par-three 16th has a small, elevated green, and young South African professional Ben Fouchee earned himself 1 000 cases of the sponsor's whisky when he made a hole-in-one here during the 1991 Bell's Cup tournament on the Sunshine Tour.

The par-four 17th runs parallel to the railway line, and the par-five 18th runs in the opposite direction, on the other side of the line. This closing hole has been toughened considerably in recent years with the addition of a water hazard just short and to the left and a large bunker to the front right of the tiny green, leaving a narrow entrance for anyone going for the flag with the second shot.

OPPOSITE: *Travelling through an avenue of pine trees, the 15th fairway gives the golfer an incomparable view of Devil's Peak.*

ROYAL CAPE GOLF CLUB

Designed by Dr Charles Molteno Murray

On entering the gates of the Royal Cape Golf Club, the immaculate grooming of the property conveys an immediate impression of proud tradition and history, as befits the position of this prestigious club. Founded in 1885, Royal Cape is the oldest golf club in South Africa, an honour it carries with justifiable pride.

Lieutenant-General Sir Henry D'Oyley Torrens arrived in Cape Town in November 1885, in command of the British troops at the Cape of Good Hope. A great golfing enthusiast, nine days after his arrival Sir Henry called a meeting at the Castle in Cape Town with the intention of starting a golf club. A letter was sent to 65 prominent Cape citizens inviting them to become members of the proposed golf club. Within a year at least 25 of them had become members of the Cape Golf Club, with Sir Henry as the club's first captain.

The first course covered nine holes at Waterloo Green, Wynberg. The club's popularity waned after the departure of Sir Henry, who left in 1888 to become Governor of Malta, where he founded the Royal Malta Golf Club. Enthusiasm was revived in 1889, however, through the efforts of a founder member, Sir David Gill, the Astronomer Royal at the Cape, who went on to become the most famous astronomer in the world.

The green of the par-five 5th hole brings this dam into play.

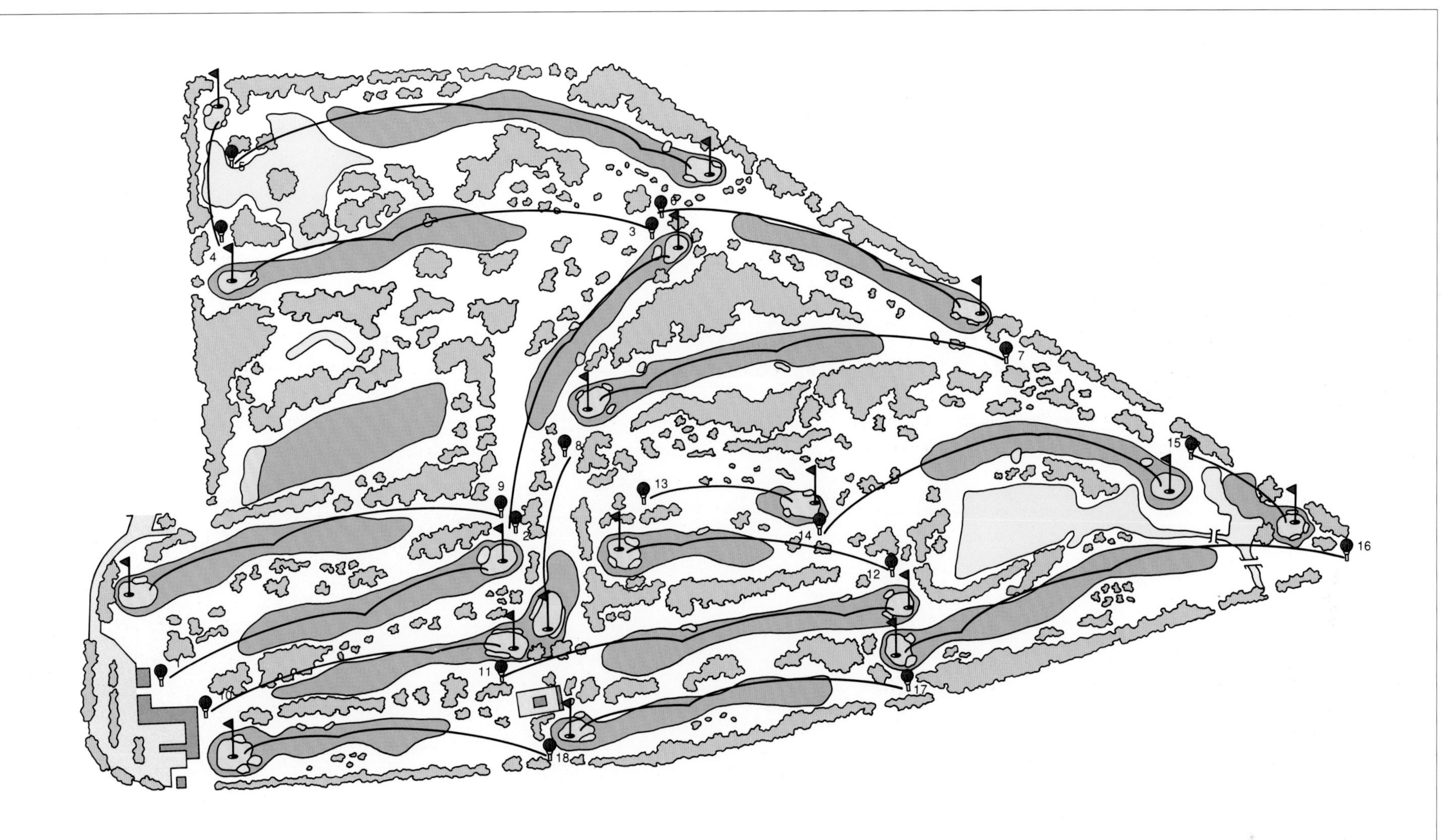

ROYAL CAPE GOLF CLUB

HOLES 18
DISTANCE 6 121 metres
PAR 72
RATING 72

HOLE	METRES	PAR	HOLE	METRES	PAR
1	367	4	10	322	4
2	341	4	11	442	5
3	433	4	12	302	4
4	131	3	13	170	3
5	491	5	14	401	4
6	341	4	15	148	3
7	460	5	16	485	5
8	171	3	17	379	4
9	385	4	18	352	4
OUT	**3 120**	**36**	**IN**	**3 001**	**36**

In 1890 the club moved to Rondebosch Common, but this proved unsatisfactory, being on public land. Rugby matches were played across the holes, and carts were driven over greens and fairways. As a result, in 1905 the land on which the present course now stands was acquired near Kenilworth racecourse, in Wynberg-Ottery on the Cape Flats. The 18-hole course opened for play a year later. The Rondebosch layout was maintained for play until 1910, so for five years the club had two courses.

The Cape Golf Club was the first South African club to be given a Royal Charter following a visit in 1910 by the Duke of Connaught, who attended the opening of the first Union Parliament.

The next 20 years were a golden era at Royal Cape as it assumed a position of pre-eminence in South African golf. A.B. Godbold, a member of Royal Cape, was president of the South African Golf Union from 1910 until 1930, and the club also provided four of the SAGU's honorary secretaries. Another member, Charles Kingsley, became the first president of the Western Province Golf Union, and later served as SAGU president. During this period the club also provided six South African Amateur champions, who between them won the title 10 times, the most famous among these being H. Gordon Stewart. Jack Watermeyer was both Amateur champion in 1940 and SAGU president during 1961-62, the only person ever to achieve this distinction. Royal Cape has a strong tradition of providing SAGU presidents, the most recent being Michael Watermeyer, whose term ended in 1992.

Although the Cape Flats course became very popular, the original layout was never entirely satisfactory because of the fact that the course had to cross the Cape Flats railway line. In 1925 the club

The 14th green features a spectacular mountain view.

The par-five 16th hole plays to a well-bunkered green.

SOUTH AFRICAN OPEN WINNERS

1910	George Fotheringham (315)
1914	George Fotheringham (299)
1923	Jock Brews (315)
1929	Archie Tosh (315)
1936	Clarence Olander (297)
1953	Jimmy Boyd (302)*
1965	Gary Player (273)
1983	Charlie Bolling (USA) (278)
1990	Trevor Dodds (285)

*Won 36-hole play-off against Otway Hayes

SOUTH AFRICAN AMATEUR WINNERS

1910	Dr E.L. Steyn
1914	Stuart McPherson
1923	William Stent
1929	Charlie Hunter
1936	Clarence Olander
1953	Roger Brews
1985	Neville Clarke

SOUTH AFRICAN STROKE PLAY WINNERS

1985	Dean van Staden (285)*

*Won play-off against David Wren

purchased new land near the clubhouse and scrapped the holes on the other side of the railway.

Dr Charles Molteno Murray, a member of the club since 1904 and one of the first people in South Africa to make a study of course design, assisted with the redesigning of the course, and what is essentially the present layout was opened in July 1928. At that time the two nines were played in reverse order to the way they are played today. Murray made a lifelong study of grasses, and was instrumental in ensuring that grass greens were planted at the Cape Golf Club course when it was opened in 1906, the first time in South Africa that grass replaced gravel greens. This encouraged other courses to follow suit, and in 1913 the SAGU ruled that their championships would only be held on courses with grass greens and tees.

In 1929 the redesigned course was chosen as the venue for the South African Open and Amateur championships, and Royal Cape has since hosted another six Opens, the most recent being in 1990.

The mountain ranges of the Cape Peninsula form a dramatic setting for this beautiful course. Although Royal Cape is situated inland, midway between the Table Bay and False Bay coasts, the wind often has to be taken into account as it can

Royal Cape Golf Club, situated in the busy suburb of Wynberg on the Cape Flats.

turn what looks like a benign parkland layout into an extremely difficult test of golf.

It was at Royal Cape that Gary Player became the first man to break 70 in all four rounds of an Open when he won the title in 1965. At that time, the course was undergoing changes to modernize it. Robert Grimsdell was commissioned to reshape the fairways and build new bunkers, which he completed in 1967. Further changes were made in 1970 to lengthen some holes. By the time the South African Open returned to Royal Cape in 1983, the course had become far more difficult. New water hazards had been added to the 14th, 15th and 16th holes to create a more challenging finishing stretch. These dams also provided the course with an ample supply of water for irrigation. In addition to other changes, bent grass replaced kweek on the greens. The effect of these changes was illustrated during the 1990 Open when only two players managed to break par for 72 holes.

The first two holes of the Royal Cape course are not unduly problematic, but the par-four 3rd is an exceptionally challenging hole. Covering a distance of 435 metres, a combination of fairway mounds, well-placed trees, and a water hazard situated about 100 metres from the green make it a hole to be approached carefully. This is one of the

most beautiful parts of the course, with several dams attracting a variety of bird species.

The short 4th is played over water to a bunkered green. The tee of the par-five 5th has been built out into one of the dams, and the water has to be carried with the tee shot. The hole curves slightly right, and the approach has to be kept left to avoid tall trees on the right. The 5th and the par-four 6th run next to the railway line, after which the course turns back to the clubhouse with the par-five 7th, which has a ditch running down the right-hand side.

The 174-metre 8th hole is a good par-three, played through an avenue of trees to a two-tiered green. Like the 4th, it is made more difficult by the fact that it is always played in a cross-wind. The 9th is an attractive par-four, with a slight dogleg-left and trees standing close to the fairway.

The 10th hole is similar to the adjoining 1st, and the 436-metre 11th is the shortest of the par-fives, with an elevated green.

The 12th hole is a lovely short par-four, with enormous pine trees flanking the left side of the fairway. The small green is closely guarded by bunkers. The 13th is another par-three, and this is followed by the trio of water holes. Only a truly bad shot brings the water hazard into play on the 14th, a boomerang-shaped hole curving right, but this hole requires precision golfing even without the intervention of the water.

On the short 15th, however, the water definitely features in play, coming right up to the front of the green, and this hole caused the professionals a considerable amount of trouble during the 1990 Open. The par-five 16th has water to the right of the fairway which narrows the driving area into a bottleneck before the hole turns to the left.

The tee of the 17th lies under giant pine trees, and the trees continue down both sides of the fairway, making this a tight driving hole. The par-four 18th is reasonably short at 340 metres, with most of the difficulties being encountered around the green.

The clubhouse overlooks the 18th green and the 1st and 10th tees. Dating back to 1924, it is more than just a home to the club – it is an integral part of the history of golf in South Africa.

OPPOSITE: *The tree-lined, par-five 7th hole returns in the direction of the clubhouse.*

The water hazard on the 15th hole extends to the front of the green.

The single-storey clubhouse, set against Table Mountain and Devil's Peak.

SISHEN GOLF CLUB

Designed by Robert Grimsdell

On the edge of the Kalahari desert, in the remote regions of the Northern Cape, lies a golf course which can be ranked with the best in the country, a rare jewel in a barren landscape. Only a small percentage of golfers in South Africa have played the Sishen course, but it has held a fine reputation since its completion in 1979. It was the last work of the late Robert Grimsdell.

Many top South African golfers hold the course in high esteem. David Frost is one of Sishen's biggest fans, but then he has a soft spot for that quiet part of the world, having met his wife Linda during a tournament there in his amateur days. The course is host to the Kalahari Classic on the Winter Tour, and many a professional has ranked the layout alongside the best in the country.

Sishen Golf Club, which belongs to Iscor, lies in the mining town of Kathu, a tranquil oasis in a forest of camel thorn *(Acacia erioloba)* trees. These trees are protected in South Africa, and provide essential shade in the desert regions. In this area, however, nearly every home has a lush, beautiful garden fed by a supply of cheap water from boreholes and the Iscor iron-ore mine. Kathu is a relat-

With the abundance of water on the course, evident here separating the 18th and 9th greens, it is difficult to believe that Sishen is situated on the edge of the desert.

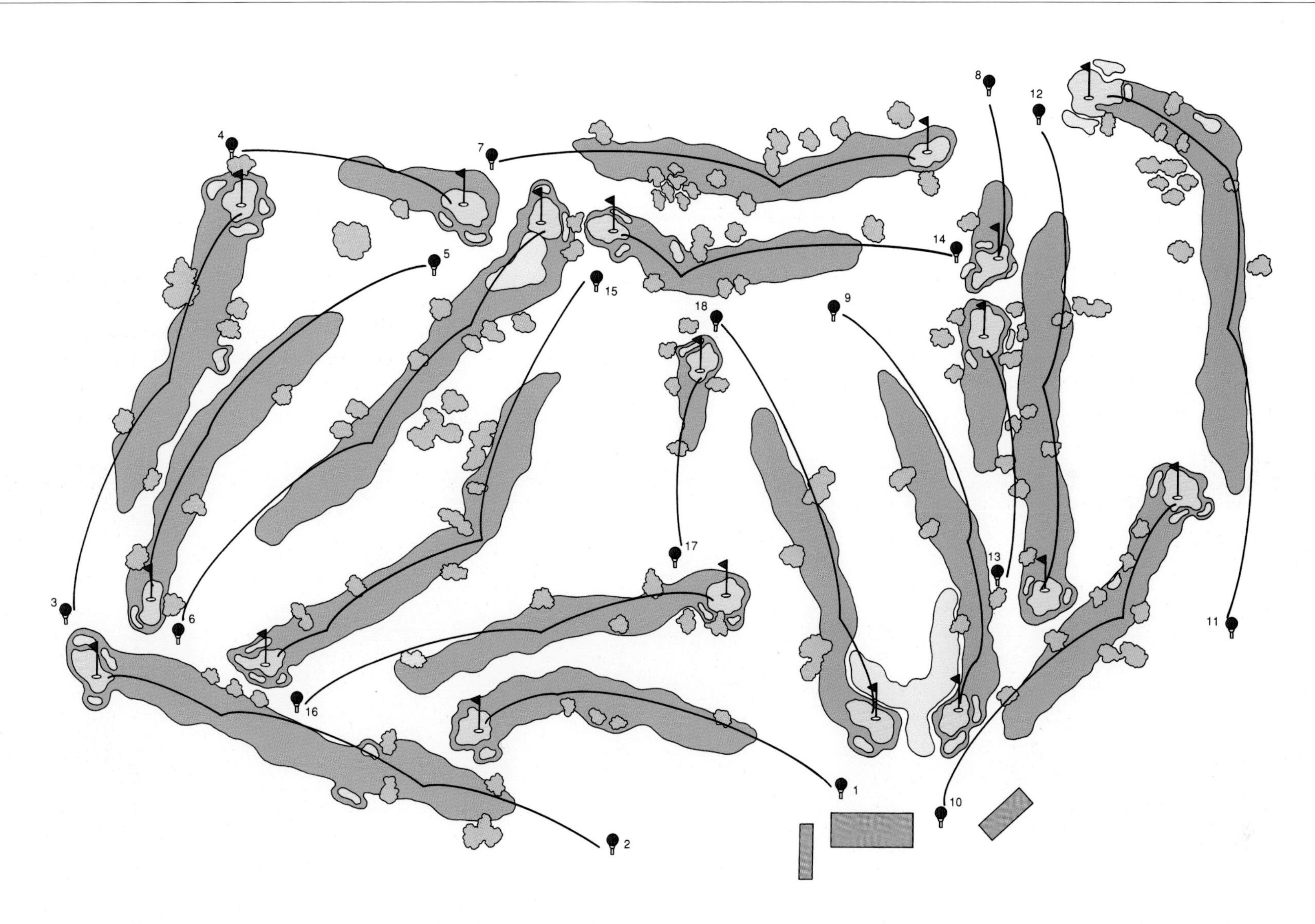

ively new town, built in the 1970s to accommodate the large mining community which had previously lived next to the mine and the ore dumps at Sishen itself. They experienced the problem of a prevailing northerly wind blowing dust from the mountainous ore dumps on to their homes, and their only solution was to build a new town situated to the north of the mine.

A round of golf at Sishen is an excellent stop-over for anyone *en route* to the Kalahari Gemsbok Park, a splendid game reserve often regarded as superior to the Kruger National Park for game viewing.

It is hard to visualize a golf course in this flat shrubland, let alone one reputed to be so good. Yet Sishen is no desert course, typical of the landscape. It was carved out of one of the largest camel thorn forests in southern Africa. There are hundreds – possibly a thousand – of these tall, beautiful trees on the course, creating a magnificent parkland layout in a serene and picturesque setting, and the birdlife is magnificent. There is such peace when playing in the late afternoon that the sound of a golf ball spinning through the still air is exaggerated.

Typical of a mine course, where there is always an abundance of water, the fairways are lush and the Outeniqua grass greens, similar to those at George Golf Club, putt as smoothly as bent grass. The excellent condition of the course cannot be doubted, as this is one of the foremost considerations when professionals rate a course. The quality of the layout is impressive and the course is one of Grimsdell's finest designs.

At 6 450 metres it is not a particularly long course, with most of the par-fours requiring only a

SISHEN GOLF CLUB

HOLES 18
DISTANCE 6 450 metres
PAR 72
RATING 72

HOLE	METRES	PAR	HOLE	METRES	PAR
1	343	4	10	342	4
2	490	5	11	520	5
3	388	4	12	420	4
4	198	3	13	210	3
5	397	4	14	326	4
6	472	5	15	468	5
7	414	4	16	399	4
8	150	3	17	165	3
9	377	4	18	371	4
OUT	**3 229**	**36**	**IN**	**3 221**	**36**

short- or medium-iron, but stretched to the back of the tees, and with pins tucked away in corners of the large undulating greens, it can be punishing. During one of the Kalahari Classic tournaments, the club decided to make the course as tough as possible for the final day in order to see how difficult it could be made to play. The professionals took one look at it and protested.

Every tee shot has to be perfectly positioned, not only to avoid the numerous camel thorn trees that stand like tall sentinels at various positions along the fairways, but to have a shot at the pin. The trees are so thick that they have the same effect on a golf ball as a brick wall – the ball plummets straight to the ground, and if it has a balata cover there may be thorns embedded in the skin. Strategically

ABOVE: *The 14th hole is a superb, short par-four, with a straight tee shot essential to set up a view of the green.*

OPPOSITE: *The brave can attempt to carry this water hazard to reach the 6th green in two strokes.*

The 8th hole: every shot has to be perfectly positioned to avoid the camel thorn trees.

The 1st green: the Outeniqua grass greens putt as smoothly as bent grass.

KALAHARI CLASSIC WINNERS	
1988	Ben Fouchee (amateur) (139 over 36 holes)
1989	Carl Cooper (204)
1990	Andre Cruse (211)
1991	Des Terblanche (208)
1992	Derek James (206)

placed bunkers present further obstacles, although the white sand has an excellent texture, having been railed all the way from Saldanha Bay.

The greens of the 9th and 18th holes are both guarded by a large water hole, as is the par-five 6th hole, where the brave long-hitter can attempt the green in two strokes. There are three short par-fours where a bogey is as easy to come by as a birdie. The 326-metre 14th is a classic hole, calling for a low long-iron off the tee to avoid overhanging branches and then a wedge or less to reach the sloping green which is tucked around a corner.

Four of the holes on the golf course are named on the scorecard after prominent members. The 18th hole is known as 'Ben', in honour of Springbok Ben Fouchee, who won the 1987 South African Amateur title at Glendower Golf Club before turning professional.

The other three holes are named after Solly Watson, Martiens Mulder and Bok Wessels, who were instrumental figures in the founding and construction of the course. Watson was the mine manager who, in the 1970s, was given a budget of R250 000 to build a nine-hole course. He called in Robert Grimsdell, one of the best architects in the business, and ended up spending R1,5-million in creating 18 outstanding holes. Wessels, a giant of a man who played golf for the Orange Free State, but would not have been out of place packing in a rugby scrum, was involved in the construction of the course and his pride in what has been achieved is obvious. Mulder was closely involved in overseeing the project, ensuring that it was built to Grimsdell's specifications.

In addition to the course, there is a practice area and a large, modern clubhouse.

OPPOSITE: *Having avoided the dense camel thorn trees lining the fairway of the 9th hole, the green needs to be approached carefully to clear the large water hazard.*

GOLF COURSE ADDRESSES

Durban Country Club
PO Box 1504, Durban 4000
Telephone: (031) 23-8282
Facsimile: (031) 23-0121

East London Golf Club
PO Box 226, East London 5200
Telephone: (0431) 35-1356
Facsimile: (0431) 35-2426

Fancourt Country Club
PO Box 2266, George 6530
Telephone: (0441) 70-8282
Facsimile: (0441) 70-7605

Fish River Sun Country Club
PO Box 232, Port Alfred 6170
Telephone: (0405) 66-1101
Facsimile: (0405) 66-1115

Gary Player Country Club
PO Box 5, Sun City, Bophuthatswana 0316
Telephone: (01465) 21000
Facsimile: (01465) 73426

George Golf Club
PO Box 81, George 6530
Telephone: (0441) 73-6116
Facsimile: (0441) 74-6191

Glendower Golf Club
PO Box 56, Bedfordview 2008
Telephone: (011) 453-1013
Facsimile: (011) 453-1013

Goldfields West Golf Club
PO Box 111, Carletonville 2500
Telephone: (01491) 81-1570

Hans Merensky Golf Club
PO Box 4, Phalaborwa 1390
Telephone: (01524) 5931
Facsimile: (01524) 85309

Houghton Golf Club
PO Box 87240, Houghton 2041
Telephone: (011) 728-7337
Facsimile: (011) 728-7349

Humewood Golf Club
PO Box 1293, Humewood 6000
Telephone: (041) 53-2137

Maccauvlei Golf Club
PO Box 82, Vereeniging 1930
Telephone: (016) 21-3196
Facsimile: (016) 21-3197

Maritzburg Country Club
PO Box 203, Pietermaritzburg 3200
Telephone: (0331) 47-1942
Facsimile: (0331) 47-1942

Milnerton Golf Club
Bridge Road, Milnerton 7441
Telephone: (021) 52-1047
Facsimile: (021) 551-5897

Mount Edgecombe Country Club
PO Box 62, Mount Edgecombe 4300
Telephone: (031) 59-5330
Facsimile: (031) 59-5330

Mowbray Golf Club
PO Box 3, Pinelands 7430
Telephone: (021) 685-3018
Facsimile: (021) 686-6008

Oppenheimer Park Golf Club
PO Box 154, Welkom 9460
Telephone: (0171) 353-2131

Roodepoort Country Club
PO Box 21488, Helderkruin 1733
Telephone: (011) 662-1990
Facsimile: (011) 662-1480

Royal Cape Golf Club
174 Ottery Road, Wynberg 7800
Telephone: (021) 761-6551
Facsimile: (021) 797-5249

Royal Durban Golf Club
PO Box 47599, Greyville 4023
Telephone: (031) 309-1373
Facsimile: (031) 309-2211

Royal Johannesburg Golf Club
PO Box 46017, Orange Grove 2119
Telephone: (011) 640-3021
Facsimile: (011) 640-1489

Selborne Country Club
PO Box 2, Pennington 4184
Telephone: (0323) 51133
Facsimile: (0323) 51811

Sishen Golf Club
PO Box 841, Kathu 8446
Telephone: (0595) 32211
Facsimile: (0595) 32855

The Wanderers Golf Club
PO Box 55005, Northlands 2116
Telephone: (011) 447-3311
Facsimile: (011) 447-1596

Wild Coast Sun Country Club
PO Box 23, Port Edward 4295
Telephone: (0471) 52799
Facsimile: (0471) 52869

INDEX

Page numbers in **bold** indicate main entries.